Including: How to Double Your Clients Without Spending One More Penny on Marketing!

THE

ULTIMATE LAW FIRM

RECLUSIVE ATTORNEY FINALLY REVEALS HOW HE CREATED A LAW FIRM THAT VACUUMS IN AN ABUNDANT SUPPLY OF NEW CASES, PURRS LIKE A FINELY TUNED AUTOMOBILE, AND GUSHES MONEY LIKE A PERSONAL OIL WELL ... WITHOUT HIM PERSONALLY HANDLING A SINGLE CLIENT!

CRAIG A. KAHN, ESQ.

Printed in the United States of America
ISBN: 978-1-63385-175-7

Word Association Publishers
205 Fifth Avenue
Tarentum, Pennsylvania 15084
wordassociation.com

TABLE OF CONTENTS

PART I: MIND TRASH

PART II: ESCAPING THE LEAD TRAP

PART III: CREATING A ROCK-SOLID FOUNDATION

THE ULTIMATE LAW FIRM

How This Book Is Structured

Introductory Matters

In this section of the book, we will address whom this book is best suited to help, what this book is about, and what experience and qualifications I have to tell you what works and doesn't work in growing a profitable law firm.

Part I: Mind Trash

In this section, we will discuss how your mind-set is the first place where success or lack thereof begins. The way you think about yourself, your practice, your clients, money, ethics, etc. all have a huge impact on how far you will go. I'm not talking about giving yourself pep talks or that somehow by just thinking good thoughts or praying that good things will happen. Instead, I'm talking about how the thoughts you have are the first step in the actions you take or don't take and how these thoughts supply the fuel for your success or failure. Although I address some common, self-limiting lawyer beliefs in this section, throughout the book, I will point out other mind-set shifts that must take place to successfully implement the ideas presented in those chapters.

Part II: Escaping the Lead Trap

In this section, we will discuss why the first step to growing your practice is *not* to get more leads. I will show you how you can make a dramatic impact on your caseload volume by working from the inside out, by getting more out of what you already have. Although it's best to have good systems, staff, and reporting in place before implementing these ideas, which I address in later chapters, my intention in putting this chapter first was to give you something exciting and tactical right up-front and after a theoretical and possibly boring chapter about mind-set.

Part III: Creating a Solid Foundation for a Better Business

You can't build a house on quicksand. You must have a solid foundation or what you build will eventually come tumbling down. In this section, we will discuss all the ways to do that from policies, procedures, systems, and scripts to technology and automation. We will discuss how to hire and fire and how to motivate and incentivize as well as what reports you should be getting so you can steer the ship.

Part IV: Taking Your Marketing to the Next Level

As you can see, this is not just another marketing book for lawyers. However, there are some very important direct-marketing principles you must follow to create the practice of your dreams. In this section, we will discuss what those principles are, how you can stand out from the crowd, and how you can get the maximum response from all your advertising.

Part V: Getting a Life and "Quitting" Your Job

This is the final piece in the ultimate law firm puzzle. In this section, we will delve into how you can stop the madness, take control of your time, and finally become the CEO of your business, not an employee of your business. This chapter puts the final touches on creating a law firm that runs without you being present on a daily basis, even without you handling a single client if you so desire.

Part VI: A Final Word

At the end of the book, I give you a short statement I wrote that encapsulates the mind-set and the principles of the entrepreneurial business owner presented herein. This document can be reviewed whenever you begin to feel like you're losing your way or your business is beating you down. This statement will motivate you to fight back and stay on course. I have found it also useful to give this statement to staff members and associates shortly after they come aboard and have them sign it to indicate they have read it just so I knew they and I were on the same page.

Finally, if you have any comments you want to share or if you think you need help along this journey, I have included a way for you to get in touch with me.

CHAPTER 1

Introduction
Who Is This Book For?

Do any of these sentences describe your thoughts and feelings on what you would like to change about your law practice?

- I want to grow the size of my firm's caseload.
- I want to take home more income from my business.
- I want more free time to take long vacations.
- I want my business to be able to operate well even when I am not present for multiple days, weeks, or even months.
- I feel like I have a job, not like the CEO or owner of a profitable business.
- I'd like to stop handling the day-to-day aspects of a full caseload and be more like the CEO of my law firm.
- I would like to cut down or eliminate the constant interruptions to my day from clients, staff, and vendors who have questions.

If you've had one or more of the above thoughts, you're reading the right book—possibly the only book you've ever read designed to help lawyers who feel like this solve these problems. It was written by a lawyer who once made all these "I wish … want … feel" statements and then actually figured out ways to make the wishes and wants come true in the real world, not in theory.

So, what type of lawyer or law firm is this book best suited to help? As you know, contrary to public perception, not all lawyers are the same. Not only do lawyers have different areas of specialization much like doctors, but they also have fundamentally different types of clients and business models. One type of lawyer obtains clients slowly over time, mostly by way of referral and relationship building. These clients feed him and his law firm various types of legal jobs. These lawyers usually bill their clients to handle these tasks using the billable hour. Typically, these clients remain with one firm for many years and that firm has enough lawyers with the proper specialization to be able to handle all its clients' needs. This type of client is usually a corporation as opposed to an individual. We will call this type of lawyer and law firm a "defense" lawyer or firm for purposes of this book.

The other type of lawyer obtains clients who have one very specific need. Many times, the lawyer has little or no relationship with this client other than during the time the lawyer is handling the need. The clients usually have little or no ability to become repeat clients; once their needs are satisfied by the lawyer, the odds of their coming back for this service are slim to none.

This is typically the only service the lawyer offers. The lawyer typically bills these clients a percentage of the recovery or a flat fee for the service performed. It's very common for these clients to be individuals as opposed to corporations. Similarly, the lawyer may obtain these clients in relatively large numbers in relatively short periods of time—there is continual churn. We will call this type of lawyer or law firm a "plaintiff's" lawyer or firm for purposes of this book.

It's this second type of lawyer and law firm that this book is primarily designed to help. If you are a defense lawyer, you may find some chapters in this book helpful to you or your practice, but most of the chapters are aimed at plaintiff lawyers and their firms.

There are concepts and ideas presented in this book that speak to solo practitioners just starting their law firms as well as more-advanced concepts designed for those who have been in business for some time. This book can be equally helpful to both types of people. For lawyers who are just starting out, this book can act as a roadmap to guide them as they grow their firms. For lawyers who have already been in business, the more-basic concepts can simply act as reminders of things they may have forgotten over time. Additionally, there should be more than enough advanced concepts in this book to provide them with significant value.

CHAPTER 2

What Is This Book About?

If you're looking for that "one thing" or that "magic bullet" that will make your law firm successful, you have the wrong book. This is book is not about one big idea that will turn your firm into a success. The major theme running throughout this book is the massive, cumulative effect many small improvements can have on your business and your life; "little hinges swing big doors," as author and marketing consultant Dan Kennedy says.

We will explore some common and many little-known and advanced strategies for you to save time, increase cases/clients, increase revenue, cut costs, reduce stress, reduce risk, and create more free time for you, the business owner. Though we also discuss how to dramatically improve your marketing, this is not another marketing book. This book is designed to cover the operation of your entire firm—from getting more leads and clients to better management of your clients and your staff and keeping track of all the numbers in a more organized and useful fashion to giving you more free time than you ever dreamed possible.

Of course, when implemented, certain ideas will have a more dramatic effect than will others, and you will want to prioritize based on those desired outcomes. However, don't lose sight of the fact that you will want to make it your goal to successfully implement as many of them as possible to have the most dramatic cumulative effect on your firm.

Just learning new ideas will not do you any good, however, unless you actually take action and implement them. The key to your success is rapid and massive action on multiple fronts simultaneously, not sequentially. This is a huge challenge for most people, especially lawyers. Their tendency is to think and plan and think and plan and think and plan before taking the first step. However, the law of inertia says it's much easier to correct course once you have the ball rolling than it is to get the ball rolling initially. You will have to resist this planning-to-death tendency and use a "ready, fire, aim" approach as opposed to "read, aim, fire" approach, as entrepreneur and business author Michael Masterson would say. You will have to get your mind right and then put in this type of effort to get the most from the ideas in these chapters and those found outside this book.

CHAPTER 3

About the Author–Why Listen to Me?

As you know, my name is Craig A. Kahn. I'm the founder and managing partner of the law firm of Kahn & Associates, L.L.C. I grew up in northeast Ohio and graduated from Shaker Heights High School in 1987. I attended Colorado State University and then Vermont Law School, where I received a master's degree and juris doctor while staying as near as I could to the ski slopes.

After graduating from law school in 1994, I wasn't sure I wanted to practice law, so I went to work for my cousins' steel and building products company in management and sales, and I handled minor legal tasks for the company.

A couple of years later, I realized I wanted to get back to the law; I actually missed reading and thinking about substantive issues and was tired of being treated like an uneducated person by customers in our showroom who had no idea I just graduated from law school with two advanced degrees. I ran across an old friend who had recently started a law firm helping consumers whose vehicles were defective. After some discussion and taking a trip to his office to see for myself, I agreed to open up the Ohio branch of his practice. Kahn & Associates was born shortly after, in 1996.

Kahn & Associates started out of a spare room in my apartment. I'd do my copying at night at a Kinko's, drive my mail to the post office, and meet clients at my father's law office. Early on, I handled every client and case myself. However, as the demand (I was creating) for my services was growing, I knew I wouldn't be able to operate much longer without any help. Fast forward a bit, and it wasn't long before I was managing a group of attorneys, paralegals, marketing people, accounting people, and various other staffers.

Since 1996, my law firm has focused almost exclusively on lemon law and warranty law. From the start, when I opened my door, I was intent on building one of the most successful practices in the country. Unlike many lawyers—and this might include you—I never had an aversion to marketing and selling my services and firm—those were not terms I was allergic to.

Over the next couple of years, my firm grew from just me to five lawyers and the staff it needed to support them, and it was handling hundreds of cases a year. Then, wouldn't you know it, the vultures started circling as word got out about what a good thing we had going. Unfortunately, over this time, multiple competitors set up shop in our market, and our caseload started to dwindle.

How I Discovered the Fortune Hidden in My Practice

I was deathly afraid of losing ground. I had a gut feeling I needed to do something different from what everyone around me was doing as well as what I was doing, so I started looking for someone outside the legal field who could look at my situation with a fresh set of eyes. I hired

Scott Hallman, a business consultant. Scott has been twice named an Inc. 500 CEO and has worked closely with some very famous motivational speakers, authors, and business consultants such as Tony Robbins, Chet Holmes, Jay Abraham, and Jay Levinson.

We dug into my entire marketing and intake system and pulled out granular details I would have never thought mattered. Some of the things Scott and I discovered were startling, such as the huge opportunity available to increase the number of our cases by reaching, meeting with, and converting more leads we were already receiving to clients versus going out and marketing for more leads. We also rewrote my ads and website landing pages to make them more consumer focused and benefit driven rather than have them simply blowing my firm's trumpet. We met and answered more of the questions running through our prospects' minds, the most important one being, *What's in it for me?* (a.k.a. WIIFM). We dramatically improved my entire intake and follow-up process and systematized them. I'll be giving more details on this later, but right now, let's just say the tide began to turn very noticeably. Our clicks increased on our ads, the number of people who submitted our form or called us increased, and the number of people who became clients doubled!

But that wasn't all we did. After our systems were perfected, we began to expand our practice in a way not done by very many plaintiff practices. Over the years, we expanded from a local practice in Cleveland to a much broader practice encompassing fifteen states. At our peak, shortly before the recession, we were fielding approximately 12,000 web submission forms and thousands more phone calls and retaining over 2,000 new clients per year!

Then It All Came Crashing Down

By the end of 2008, we'd had enough experience in some of our states to decide we'd had enough of them. The volume of cases was just too small to warrant a dedicated full-time attorney and office in certain states. In other states, the litigation environment for consumers was too much to overcome for the relatively few bucks involved in each matter. Some of our offices were losing money or just breaking even. So at the end of 2008, our new pro forma projections showed that at current new case and settlement figures, if we eliminated all the costs associated with those offices in five specific states, 2009 would look rosy.

But it turned out that a slow cancer was spreading beneath our feet as new auto sales were dropping significantly during that year. By 2009, they were on the verge of a historic low—from a peak of 17 million in 2005 to a low of almost 9 million in 2009, close to a 50 percent decline! (See figure 1 on following page.)

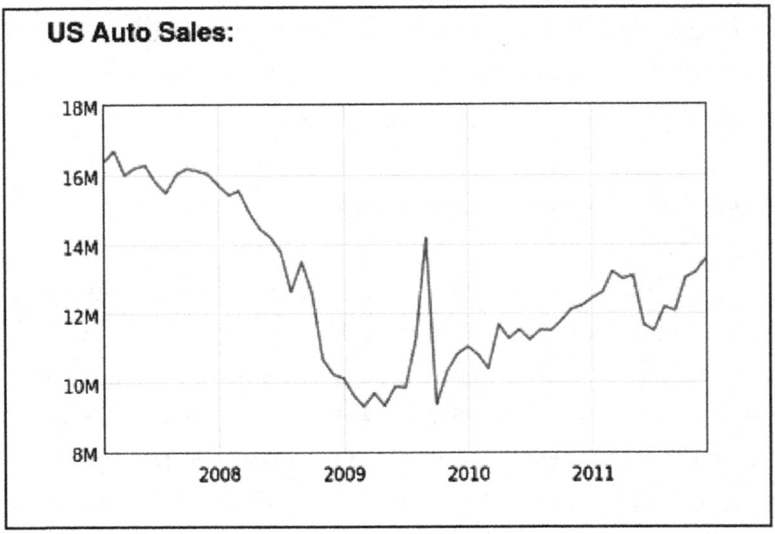

Figure 1: US Auto Sales

And Then the Other Shoe Dropped

Chrysler filed for Chapter 11 Bankruptcy on April 30, 2009. GM did the same on June 1 of that year. We were floored. We'd been planning for rough waters, but we had no idea things would fall so far so fast.

We spent the next two years in a self-imposed Chapter 11 reorganization plan. We analyzed all our revenue streams and expenses to determine what to do. We had seven managers in the firm handling marketing, IT, HR, paralegals, attorneys, and so on. Instead of simply firing many of them, we made them part-time with notice so they could find other jobs, which eventually they all did.

Next, we gave all our attorneys the support they needed to set up offices on their own. The arrangement was that we would continue to pay for marketing to generate leads and cases that we would then refer to them on a fee-sharing basis. And something amazing happened. I prepared mini pro formas for the attorneys showing their likely revenue, expenses, and net profit. When I showed them how much they could earn with a staff person on their payrolls and how much they would earn without a staff person, they all opted to go it alone. When they were working at our firm, they had to have staff helping them, but when they saw the expenses that would be coming out of their own pockets, they somehow found ways to get everything done by themselves. The lesson here as you grow is don't immediately assume your staff is right when they tell you they can't get all the work done and need more help.

We also took what we were good at—our online marketing—and duplicated this co- counsel business model with more practice areas. We picked two or three we thought would work well using our systems and provide reasonably quick settlements. We contacted partners who were specialists in those areas of law and offered to do the same thing we did with our own attorneys. We would bring in the cases at our expense, send them to these attorneys, and share the fees. We made websites for personal injury cases, Fair Debt Collection Practices Act (FDCPA) cases, Fair Credit Reporting Act (FCRA) cases, and employment law/overtime cases. That way, we hoped that at least some of these would help us quickly replace lost income without having to become experts in all these practice areas, which would have taken us much longer.

In 2011, we got more aggressive with the FDCPA practice area and began to learn it ourselves. With the help of the same friend who got me into the lemon-law business originally, who was going through the same struggle and added FDCPA cases to his firm, we began to take on our own cases without referring them out. This helped us diversify our firm so we weren't so dependent on lemon law. We got to the point that 50 percent of our files were FDCPA.

Eventually, our reporting showed us that we weren't making much net income from our lemon law co-counsel arrangements and informed those attorneys we could no longer pay for the marketing to generate cases for them. However, because our websites were ranked organically, we would continue to receive free leads and cases that we would continue to send them so the drop was not immediate and dramatic.

What the Firm Looks Like Today

Fast forward to today and we are back to one main office and the only cases we handle, we handle ourselves with no outside counsel. Today, our office handles cases from all over Ohio and Michigan, and we're seeing a rebound in our lemon-law practice area as new car sales returned to prerecession levels.

Though my job hasn't changed very much over the years, I now spend much less time on it. My role is to manage my team of dedicated attorneys who are responsible for the day-to-day handling of our clients' cases; I get involved when difficult questions come up with cases or strategy issues need addressing.

I spend my time educating the market of consumers and ensuring that our firm delivers on its promises. My main areas of focus are setting goals, managing from 10,000 feet, making major policy and procedural changes, steering the ship toward our goals, and reviewing file audits to ensure things are moving forward. I review reports on our key metrics, change our marketing strategies and approaches as necessary, go over accounting reports, work on special projects to improve the firm and its systems, handle high-level HR tasks such as benefits, bonuses, final hiring and firing decisions, and so on. How much time do you think that takes me per week? About five to ten hours—one or two hours a day. If we have any big projects or decide to expand, my time would spike up temporarily while working on that project or goal.

All the day-to-day casework, the "in the trenches" work—from intake to trial to check collection, bookkeeping, etc.—is handled by the people who work on these day-to-day matters following the systems I've put in place.

I've become the CEO of a business that provides me an almost passive income stream rather than the owner of a business who also has a 9-to-5 job there. Typically in the latter scenario, if lawyers were to extract themselves from their jobs at the firm, they might not be able to take any income from their businesses. If they were to retire, their firms might not be in a position to provide any income to them. That's the difference between earned income and passive income as well as the difference between having salary income versus owning income-producing assets.

So what do I do with the rest of my time? I use it to diversify my income stream, spend more time with my family, on vacations and on the golf course. I've become a bit of what some people call a serial entrepreneur. (More on that later too.)

Through this process, I've discovered that lawyers spend very little time learning good sales (yes, I know lawyers hate using that word!) strategies, and marketing principles because the subliminal message coming from the older generation is that those aren't worthy pursuits for those in our profession. I also learned that most lawyers just look around and copy what everyone else is doing. However, if you do only what everyone else does, you will by definition be average.

All the while, I've continued to look outside our industry for ideas that could be ethically incorporated into our firm. I read at least one book a month on marketing and sales, am a member of a national marketing organization, at various times have a business coach, and participate in a mastermind group.[1] I'm also a contributing author to a book with internationally known marketing guru Dan Kennedy, author of *The Ultimate Success Secret*. I practice what I preach; even today, I continue to educate myself and experiment with techniques from some of the best marketing and business minds in the world.

Now, I want to share what I've learned over all these years to help you reach your goals and live the life of your dreams. That's the reason I wrote this book.

PART I

MIND TRASH

CHAPTER 4

Changing Your Mind-Set
Lawyer First, Businessperson Second, or Vice Versa?

Do you consider yourself a lawyer first and a businessperson second? Do you consider your law firm a professional practice or a business that offers legal services? Making these distinctions requires a subtle but critical mind-set shift. If you want your law practice to do better, examine your mind-set about this.

Have you ever heard yourself saying you can't do something because you're a lawyer? Or you can't because the public perception of lawyers is such and such and they would expect you not to do such and such? Or even the dreaded, I can't do that because it doesn't look or appear "professional"? Many of these beliefs are simply in your head, not in the heads of others. They are excuses for not taking action or shying away from any form of risk taking. They oftentimes hold the lawyer back from trying new things and end up holding the law firm back from being a successful business. They are what motivational speaker, author, and life coach Lee Milteer calls "mind trash." I've found that thinking about law firm business issues and strategies from the mind-set of a businessperson first and a lawyer second is an absolute must if you want to create something unique and highly successful.

It's my position that for you to get the most out of this book and make the most of your practice, you'll likely have to change your mind-set about one or more issues. This isn't just a book about tactics; your ability to succeed with your business starts with your mind-set. No, I'm not talking about imagining and hoping things will magically happen; I'm talking about the way you think about the practice of law, industry norms, your peers, your relationship with money, how you view your staff, and even the big bad bar association.

Let's go over a few of the mind-set shifts in this chapter. We'll touch on more of these throughout this book.

CHAPTER 5

Are You Scared of Your State Board of Ethics?

Do you find yourself deciding whether to move forward with a plan or idea by asking whether it's ethical? Of course, as lawyers, we all have to ask that question. But I've found that where lawyers draw the line on what's ethical and what isn't can be vastly different, and that can have a huge impact on their relative successes.

We all know there's a grey area in all areas of the law even when it comes to whether a specific set of facts or action taken is ethical or not. I know of lawyers who have interpreted the rules in ways that would cripple your business. For example, one lawyer told me that because we cannot advertise our firm under a trade name, we had to do something about our vanity 800 number. No, not in our ads, but with the way it's displayed on the recipient's phone screen!

Another lawyer I worked with was afraid to force a defendant to answer the complaints we were filing against a manufacturer because the defense attorney was on the board of ethics for the state. So there we were—our clients' cases stuck at the pleading stage with no reasonable offers to settle, but the attorney was so petrified of the defense attorney's ethics status that he refused to make the defendant answer the complaints or file motions for default if it wasn't done in a timely fashion. That lawyer was definitely on the wrong bus (more about that later). My point is that if you take some of these rules to the extreme, you'll end up crippling your practice and getting an ulcer to boot.

CHAPTER 6

The Bar Association Isn't Your Friend

The uncomfortable truth is, if you're in private practice, the bar association isn't your friend. Many of its rules are simply detriments to your ability to make the most of your business. One of the biggest mental hurdles many lawyers must clear is how they view the bar and the rules governing lawyers whether explicit or aspirational. If you come from the perspective of a purist, a traditionalist, you'll find many of my suggestions in this book to be antithetical to your beliefs. But the fact is that many of the rules the bar association clings to are grounded in the past. As with statutory law, they typically lag behind the fast-moving world we live in.

This is especially true when it comes to how lawyers can advertise their services. At one point not that long ago, lawyer advertising was completely prohibited! Yes, as Professor Thomas Morgan put it:

> The organized bar traditionally took the position that a lawyer was not permitted to actively publicize his services. In effect, it was presumed that every lawyer had an estab-

> lished clientele, or that a lawyer's reputation for good work would inevitably lead others to seek out the lawyer's services. Under this approach, direct publicity for lawyers was strictly controlled.[2]

Then, in Bates v. State Bar of Arizona, 433 U.S. 350 (1977), the seminal U.S. Supreme Court Case on lawyer advertising, the Court ruled that lawyer advertising was commercial speech entitled to protection under the First Amendment and couldn't be banned. The State Bar of Arizona argued it wanted to maintain a certain air of "professionalism" among lawyers as justifying its ban on lawyer advertising. Advertising, the state bar asserted, would "undermine the attorney's sense of dignity and self-worth," "erode the client's trust in the attorney" by exposing an economic motive for representation, and "tarnish the dignified public image of the profession."

But in ruling that Arizona's total ban on lawyer advertising violated First Amendment free speech, the Court explained that lawyer advertising was commercial speech that would serve significant social interests by informing the public of the availability, nature, and prices of products and services. The Court said that would make legal services more accessible to the public and thus improve the overall administration of justice. The Court rejected the tradition of lawyers not advertising as a historical anachronism that had created higher barriers to entry into the legal profession and functioned to "perpetuate the market position of established attorneys."

The Court reiterated that states were still permitted to ban "false, deceptive, or misleading" advertising by lawyers; to regulate the manner in which lawyers could solicit business in person; to require warnings and disclaimers on lawyer advertising to assure that the public was not misled; and impose other reasonable restrictions on the time, place, and manner of lawyer advertising.[3]

As more and more lawyers are coming out of law schools and into the marketplace, the necessity for lawyers to market their services to prospective clients has never been greater. As a result, every so often, someone refuses to abide by one of the rules or challenges a rule in court, and then you hear about another onerous, outdated advertising ethics rule falling by the wayside. This all stems from the holding in Bates. What many lawyers who are petrified of the bar don't realize is that they have constitutional protections that can supersede the bar's authority over them when the bar overreaches.

Despite this ruling, however, many lawyers are still dealing with a host of ethics rules that have a stifling effect on business growth and innovation. Here are just some examples.

Advertising Rules

- You cannot compare your services to another lawyer's services.
- In many states, you cannot (or until very recently could not) use testimonials or list past verdicts or settlements.
- You cannot use the words *expert, specialist, free,* and *best* among others.
- In some states, you cannot use certain sounds in your ads!
- You cannot have telemarketers call your prospects from a targeted list.
- You cannot use a trade name.
- You have to put certain disclaimers, contact information, and other words or sentences into your ads and letters and even on your envelopes no matter what the size of the ads and even though they vary from your message.
- You may have to submit to the bar, for its approval, every new ad or change to your ads or website before you publish them (and in some states pay a fee!).
- You can't send letters to certain people unless you know they've been served or some other prequalifying event, or you must wait some prescribed period of time before doing so.

Other Rules

- You cannot pay referral fees to nonlawyers or other businesses that refer clients to you.
- You cannot split fees with a nonlawyer or another business that refers clients to you.
- You cannot have a nonlawyer as an equity partner in your business.
- The licensing system prevents or impairs your ability to have a national or multistate practice.
- Nonlawyers on your staff are restricted by unauthorized practice of law rules as to what they can and cannot do no matter how talented they are if they don't have a license.
- You have to defend yourself and expose your personal or proprietary information in writing against even the most baseless allegations made to the bar association against you by disgruntled clients or law firm competitors!
- And on and on ...

About the only thing that is probusiness in most rules of ethics is the concept that you must zealously represent your client—i.e., you should do a good job, and that's good business. The rest of the items I've listed above are all small impediments to doing what you want to do as a business owner to improve the profitability of your firm. The bar has no interest in making you more profitable. When was the last time you saw a continuing legal education seminar that focused on making your law firm more profitable, becoming better at salesmanship and marketing, or opening multiple offices?

Unfortunately, because of the number of attorneys we've had and the volume of cases we've handled, I've been through more than enough of these to have learned this and how the bar associations deal with them. I never, ever intentionally violate a rule of ethics with the hopes it will never come to light. A huge reason why is that these things have a way of coming to light, and it usually starts with a client complaint. Once a client complains to the bar association, the bar ends up peeking underneath the hood at all kinds of things you'd never expect them to. They'll round up copies of your direct-mail pieces, ads, agreements, and other documents, talk to the client, look at your website, on and on—basically go on a fishing expedition. While the client might have simply complained that you charged too much, the bar could add more issues than that to the inquiry. My opinion is this: if you're not stealing money and not completely neglecting your clients' cases and you write a reasoned response and participate in their inquiry, they'll dismiss the matter quickly or simply ask you to make a change to your ads, letters, agreement, and so on. Once you do that, the matter goes away.

I often tell the attorneys I work with that the reason I'm not overly concerned when I get one of these letters from the bar is that I know I'm not doing anything nefarious that would warrant any kind of sanction. I am not stealing money or neglecting client matters—two things that will surely get you in hot water. If I have done anything that got me into or past the grey area, it was inadvertent and a good-faith interpretation of the rules. It's a big step for the bar to suspend someone's livelihood, and it simply wouldn't invest the resources to try to do that for something that isn't a serious matter. And it knows it can be a fight. I can put up a defense, and it will have to take the case to what is in essence a trial and prevail. I don't think I'm the kind of attorney the bar would invest significant resources in trying to remove.

CHAPTER 7

Lawyers Are Allowed to Have Fun and Make Money

It took me many years to become clear on whether it was acceptable for me to concentrate on actually making money in my practice. There were constant negative influences pressuring me to forget about the money and focus solely on my clients' interests.

For example, when I started my consumer law practice, I occasionally used one successful attorney as a sounding board. I remember her telling me I needed to hide my desire for attorney's fees from the court; I had to make sure I was the one in court wearing the white hat, an attorney whose only interest was benefitting my client. Otherwise, I risked "pissing off" the court and getting my fee petition denied or my fees substantially reduced. That's the kind of thinking I want to warn you about. Why should you or I be ashamed that we need to be paid for our work? I want my expertise and my time to be valued and valued highly. The way we're recognized for our value in America is by the money we receive for our services! It's also how we keep score.

In our business, attorney's fees are recoverable from the defendant in addition to the plaintiff's damages. Naturally then, most firms take on these cases with the intention of billing hours. However, we continually run into resistance before the court during settlement talks at a hearing. The judge will say something like, "So you're going to hold up this settlement over your attorney's fees?" In other words, the plaintiff is being paid a reasonable amount but the amount we're asking for isn't acceptable. It's not uncommon to have $10,000 or more in billable hours but be pressured to take $2,000 or less for them.

This got me thinking how many law practices have no control over what they want to be paid. Most businesses know that if they sell 500 widgets, they'll make $5,000. Not us lawyers. We have to sell the widgets and then resist the pressure to cut our prices to resolve a case and make our clients happy. I once heard someone say that not only is it acceptable for lawyers to focus on making money, it's also actually in the clients' best interests; it's imperative. This is simply because if you're not making money, you won't be providing services to your clients for very long. You cannot hire and retain the best talent for your clients, buy the latest time-saving technologies, pay for the best experts, investigators, and vendors and many other things a business needs to continue to provide the best service if you are not making money. This is the proper mind-set to have if you want your firm to be successful.

In the next chapter, I'll share with you how to double your cases without spending any additional money on marketing. Interested in that?

PART II

ESCAPING THE LEAD TRAP

CHAPTER 8

How to Double Your Clients without Spending One More Penny on Marketing!

So you want to grow your law firm and increase your revenue. What do you do first? You try to get more leads so you can get more clients and cases, right? Since you're already getting as many leads and cases as you can from your current marketing budget, this would mean spending more money on marketing, right? Wrong! That's not what you want to do to get more clients or cases ... yet. Most firms can literally double their current clients and cases without spending an additional dime on advertising. That sounds hard to believe, but that was exactly what I did.

As I mentioned earlier, at one time, my competition increased and my cases started to dwindle. My business consultant and I dug into my entire marketing and intake system and discovered the huge opportunity I had to increase our cases by simply engaging more of the prospects I was already receiving. We rewrote my ads and website landing pages to be more consumer focused and benefit driven rather than focused on the firm. Then we substantially improved my entire intake and follow-up process.

After making these changes, the tide began to turn.

Our clicks increased on our ads, the number of people who submitted our form or called increased, the number of people who then became clients increased, and we doubled our number of cases without spending a penny more on marketing or personnel.

Let's take a simple marketing funnel that begins with a website. Here are the steps most prospects go through before becoming clients (with sample numbers and conversion rates). You start with:

1. impressions/views, then
2. clicks on your ads, then
3. forms filled out on your site/chats engaged / phone numbers called, then
4. prospects reached and meaningful conversations had, then
5. appointments scheduled (or not ready yet), then
6. appointments kept (show rate), then
7. clients gather more information or attorney-client agreement presented, then
8. agreements signed,
9. then cases filed, then
10. full fees paid!

A sample funnel before being optimized would look something like the one in figure 2 on the following page.

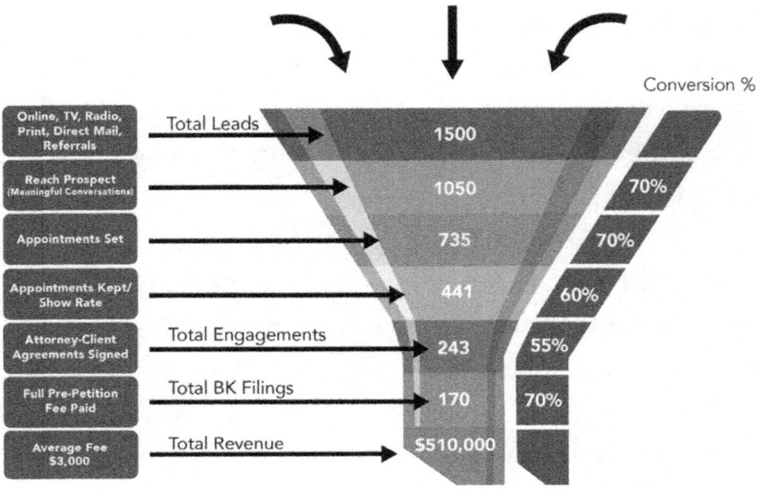

Figure 2: Marketing Funnel before Optimizing

At each step in this process, a certain percentage of people move on to the next step while a certain percentage fall out of the funnel; some people refer to this as having "holes in your bucket."

Figure 3 represents a sample of what your marketing funnel would look like after making improvements to your systems. Do you see what happens? In the before picture (figure 2), you have 170 bankruptcy filings and $510,000 of revenue per year. In the after picture (figure 3), you would have 238 bankruptcy filings and $714,000 of revenue per year with the same ad budget! How is that possible, you ask? If you look at the new conversion rate column on the far right of figure 3, you can see that making small improvements to each of these numbers starts an incredible compounding effect the further you get down the funnel.

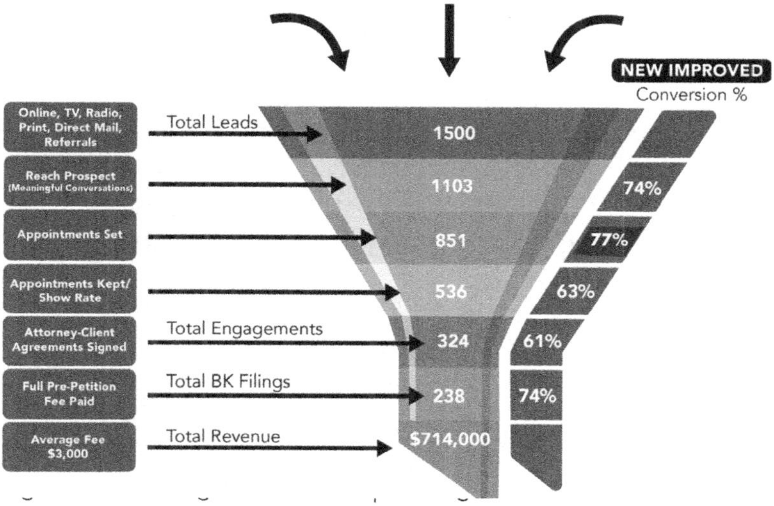

Figure 3: Marketing Funnel after Optimizing

We had an even more dramatic effect on our numbers, literally doubling our caseload, because our conversion rate from appointment to new client was an abysmal 27 percent when we started.

Keep in mind that these funnels leave out any increases you may make in conversion rates at the ad level. For example, online, this would be by increasing the number of clicks on your ads and the number of people who go from click-to-call or click-to-email. These funnels start with leads received by your firm. Improving those conversion rates would have a substantial effect on the total bankruptcy filings and revenue as well.

We found a couple things at my firm that were instrumental in boosting these numbers. First, by analyzing the data, we discovered we were reaching people by phone at almost double the rate we were reaching people who had only submitted a web form with an email address. We had allowed anyone who filled out our web form to insert their phone number as an option, so we never reached many of these leads. We changed that to requiring a phone number, and the number of people we were able to reach after that went up dramatically with almost no loss in the total number of web forms we received.

Follow-Up

Second, our follow-up was sporadic if we did any at all. This is the biggest mistake for not only law firms but also for almost every business we come in contact with as consumers. At first, I thought I'd just be annoying people; I figured if they wanted to do business with us, they would. However, when you analyze the numbers, you don't have to guess.

We established our baseline conversion rates at various steps in the process before implementing the improved follow-up system, and then we looked at the new conversion rate. We figured that if people had been annoyed by our follow-up process, the numbers would have dropped. But the numbers shot up like a rocket! We'd hear comments such as, "Thank you for following up with me. I was busy and forgot …" or "I lost the document. Please send again …"

We learned that people appreciated our follow-up; we demonstrated to them that we really did care about them and their cases and wanted to handle them. By following up consistently, we demonstrated that we weren't flakey—we were professional and organized. We gained some consistency credit with our prospects by applying gentle but continual pressure.

Make It Easy to Do Business with You

Third, we studied our process from the consumers' point of view and tried to make it as easy to do business with us as we could. If they didn't have to come to the office, we didn't require it. If we could help gather documents for them, we did that. If it meant cutting out scary language from the agreement (there to protect us in only 1 out of 100 cases) and substantially shortening it, we did. We encouraged prospects to submit an electronic signature or a faxed or scanned copy of their signature on our engagement letter instead of waiting for paper copies to come by snail mail. We did everything we ethically could to increase the conversion rate.

What we learned was that by focusing on each of the holes in our bucket and brainstorming ways to improve our scripts, systems, and processes, we could improve each of them by a minimum of 5 percent. I'm not talking about a 30 percent or a 50 percent improvement; you need a mere 5 percent to make a huge impact on a cumulative basis as demonstrated by the funnel in figure 3!

How much more money and how many more staff people do you think it takes to improve your existing systems? Typically, unless a firm is grossly understaffed and everyone is bursting at the gills, these improvements will require no more staff. Some of these improvements may require a modest investment in better cloud software, but typically, we're talking less than $300 per month for the software. Would you spend a few hundred dollars a month extra to double your caseload? That's a no-brainer.

Ask yourself how much one additional client or case is worth on average to your firm. You'll then know how much it's costing you to let one of these slip through the cracks of your system every month. You can see by the graphs above that the cost of doing nothing is dramatic.

Spending more money to find more new leads is foolish until you first identify and then plug all the holes in your bucket and optimize your marketing funnel. Why spend more money so you can pour more new leads into a leaky bucket? You're paying for leads that are slipping through your fingers. Once you stop that from happening, you'll have significantly more clients and cases. Then you can add the new money coming in to increase your marketing budget to generate even more leads. The difference will be that due to an improved system, you'll know the money is well spent and nothing's slipping through your fingers.

Next, let's discuss how to cement these changes into your firm with systems, procedures, and scripts.

PART III

CREATING A ROCK-SOLID FOUNDATION

CHAPTER 9

Externalize the Knowledge

Policies, Procedures, and Systems

It's Monday morning, and you're consumed by what you need to get done that day and what you want to get done for the upcoming week. You race to your office building, go up to your office, open the door, and turn on the light. You throw down anything in your hands, go to pull out your chair to sit down and whoa, hold everything. There's is a white envelope with handwriting on it addressed in your name. If this has ever happened to you, you already know what's inside. If it hasn't, you're about to get what is likely a very unwelcome surprise. One of the key players on your team is quitting! You have two weeks to find and train a replacement. "Two weeks?" you say. "That's not enough time to even find someone suitable, let alone have the person leaving train them. And what about all that stuff that only Jenny knows how to do? How will we manage to function after she leaves?"

Now what? Your day has just been ruined. Unless, of course, you were afraid to fire this person and this is welcome news. However, you still have the same problem of finding and training someone in short order. And I'm betting this entire task is about to fall on your shoulders.

But how would you feel if you had an assistant who knew how to find the right person—what ads to use, where to post them, how to involve your team in looking for referrals, how to screen resumes, conduct phone interviews, throw out the bad apples, and set up appointments for you with just the cream of the crop? You'd meet with two or three finalists, pick one, and make an offer. The day the person starts, your assistant gives him or her all the paperwork, gets it to accounting, files the rest, and updates your databases.

Whenever your new hires arrive, someone gives them your training manual including videos that describe how to handle every aspect of the job, how the software works, how to answer common questions, on and on. You give this to them, tell them to read it thoroughly and/or watch these videos, and give them a training buddy to coach them through their questions.

The training buddy has a spreadsheet with all the key areas of the job the new hire has to learn, and the training buddy fills it out after verifying through inspection that the new staff member has mastered this or that section. Your only job is to check the spreadsheet for indications of progress and answer any hard questions.

How would you feel if you had all that ready to go the next time someone left you a note on a Monday morning? It would still be no fun, but I bet you'd feel a whole lot more in control and a whole lot less panicked if you had this already in place. This is just one of the many reasons you should have documented systems, procedures, and scripts in place. When they are, you'll know you will end up with a person well trained in the way you want things done regardless of how it's done elsewhere. There should be a way that you do things at your firm regardless of how anyone else did it anywhere else. This should be the best way as you have determined, and it should always be subject to ongoing improvement and change. But at any given time, you need to have a way you do it, and everyone must do it that way. Without this, you cannot deliver consistent service and have a predictable business with predictable cash flow.

I call this "externalizing" the knowledge. I know you've heard, "I don't know what I'd do if Susy were to leave. She knows how to do so many key functions here that no one else knows how to do." That's not a safe situation for you, your family, and your employees to be in. But it isn't an inescapable situation. All you need to do is explain to Suzy the precarious position you're in due to this situation. It's not that you might fire her, but what if disaster strikes?

With her and everyone else's help, you create policy and procedure manuals for the benefit of the whole firm. I am not taking about some giant formal manual with thousands pages of black and white fine print. I mean very visual stand-alone documents with words and screen shots and/or videos that show someone the steps to take to follow your systems. When they are compiled in a windows folder on your computer and/or in a physical binder, I refer to this collectively as a policy and procedure manual.

You don't want someone walking out the door with key information in his or her head. And you don't want to divert your staff members' time and attention from their primary jobs to training new people on their jobs. They'll be able to train themselves on much of it by simply following the manuals and videos. They are also useful to refer back to when someone forgets a step and needs reminding. All your staff needs to do is simply document (on a spreadsheet or screen-capture video or both) how they're already performing their day-to-day tasks. A good place to start is with the simple tasks so everyone gets practice in how this will work and how you want it to look. Then you can move on to more-complicated tasks and procedures. You can schedule regular meetings with everyone to see progress, answer questions, and so forth. It can actually be a fun break from the monotony of their everyday work.

Scripts

Imagine a few months after your new paralegal starts. You check your reports and see that the monthly new client number is down 25 to 50 percent. Is one of the marketing channels not working? Is it a change in the broader economy? Is it something your new paralegal is doing or saying? Uh oh. How can you figure out what happened?

Assuming you have reports on your leads, you might be able to eliminate the marketing channels. Assuming you now have a semi-automated follow-up system, you can check to see if the manual tasks are being done. If both of these check out, then what? More questions go through your mind. How did she ask for appointments or explain the process or the engagement letter? How did she handle questions about fees and costs? If there was no script for this, no best practices, you have no way of knowing if your new assistant is doing it the way your previous person did.

This is exactly why you need to have your firm's knowledge externalized now, while you have the staff on-board who are doing it well. Once it's put down on paper or in a video or audio format, you've captured it. That way, when key staff members leave for whatever reason, your proprietary systems don't walk out the door with them.

I know most people cringe at even the mention of a script, but we all use scripts every day in our practices without even knowing it. Most of us will naturally try to come up with the best way to answer a question and repeat it to different people in pretty much the same way every time. When you're talking with existing clients and answering common questions, do you come up with different answers every time you are asked one of those questions? Or do you have what you think is the best general answer to those questions memorized and say it roughly the same way each time? Well my friends, that's all I mean when I say a script. You just probably have never put it down on paper and worked on improving it.

A common objection you'll hear from your staff when you discuss scripts with them is that they want to sound natural, not robotic. "But I don't want it to sound too mechanical," they say. "Scripts are canned, cold, and unprofessional. I need to be able to just wing it." I say this: all the people using a script can personalize it with their own filler words, cadence, accents, and so on. Tell them to go ahead and be natural—make the script their own—but make sure to use the key words and phrases and follow the order of the script. Certain key phrases and buzzwords must be used every time and in a certain order every time they answer a question. Otherwise, they're winging it in a bad way, and the results will be different depending on the person giving the answer. That's not how successful businesses are run. A successful business relies on a system that produces the same result no matter who's running it! Yes, just like McDonalds. Actors memorize scripts; when they act, they don't read them and it comes out sounding very natural. That's what you want from your team.

We all use scripts because they're useful. You want to create scripts for everyone in your firm for important conversations. There should be scripts for things such as:

- answering the phone
- conducting the intake process from screening the client to getting the engagement signed
- answering common objections, misconceptions, and FAQs
- explaining why settlement offers are good or bad
- collecting fees owed
- end-of-case conversations that promote goodwill and encourage referrals

- asking the court to rule a certain way on an issue that commonly arises in your practice
- any other key function to the successful operation of your firm

Don't just decree these scripts from on high; work with your team on coming up with them; take advantage of what they have learned. Have your team write down what questions they get and what answers they give. Add to this list yourself. Then have a few one-hour meetings with the team to explain what you're aiming for and brainstorm with them on what your collective best answers should be. Put them up on the board and get acceptance, buy-in, from everyone. If they realize they're an important part of this process, they'll be much more likely to use scripts without objection. You should also do some role-playing with the team members until everyone is comfortable with the new scripts.

CHAPTER 10

Automate, Automate, Automate!

Leveraging Technology and the Cloud for Maximum Productivity

A big part of systems and procedures involves utilizing technology that will allow you to perform daily tasks with the least amount of staff and get more done in less time. People are a law firm's biggest expense, so the more you can accomplish with the fewest people, the more net profit you'll enjoy.

Over the years, I've interviewed hundreds of people for different jobs at our law firm. I'm always amazed at the horror stories I hear about the places where they're working. I hear about bad owners who provide no direction to their teams and don't even pay them on time; it's pathetic to hear people tell me that they spend hours a week looking for the right file so they can find the name of the adjuster to call regarding settlement! That's the height of inefficiency, and there's no excuse for it in today's technological society.

Every law firm must have a practice management software program of some kind that organizes files, the people on the files, status notes, and the stage each file is in. Dozens of such programs are out there, and many now are completely cloud-based for a reasonable monthly fee.

The Cloud

I want to make sure we're all caught up on the concept of the cloud. When I started my law firm, the model most used was getting individual computers with software loaded onto each computer. When you got enough computers, you bought a server—a very large computer all the other computers pointed to; it was the hub of the wheel, and all the other computers were at the ends of each spoke.

The idea was to take certain programs and all the data being produced by all the computers and centralize it so everyone could have access to the same information. The downside to all this was that all your equipment and software quickly became obsolete and you had to pay for expensive upgrades. And I mean everything—the computers, the software, and the servers themselves; the servers are very expensive to replace.

Furthermore, you needed IT help to fix all the things that went wrong with this network and help set it up whenever you had someone new start or leave. You also had to manage the licenses, security and bug updates, and patches and perform regular maintenance. It became very difficult to budget as some years you might have fewer issues than others, and when hardware breaks, that's a big blow.

The cloud solves some of these problems; you pay a flat amount per month based on the services you need much as you do for gas or electricity. So instead of having a server and software in your closet that you own and maintain, someone else owns the server and software; it's in their closet, and they maintain it! You pay for as much as you play, so to speak; it's much easier to budget that way. Your spend is constant each month, and you have the latest version of all the software you use. You never have to worry about unexpected expenses.

Practice Management Software

Okay, so back to practice management software. The basic tasks you want your practice management software to perform are:

1. organizing all your files by file number, type, and name
2. instantly finding the names and contact information of everyone associated with that file.
3. allowing anyone who touches the file to see the latest status notes and add status notes.
4. prompting you for the next task or appointment due on the file automatically
5. keeping a calendar of appointments viewable on a central calendar and with each appointment connected to and viewable inside a specific file
6. allowing you to bill and keep track of your time during the day

7. allowing you to save a chain of common tasks and appointments that can be added to each new file without having to recreate the individual items each time a new matter is opened (similar to a template)—very important!
8. letting you run basic reports on demand

You also want the ability to create templates in the software that can be merged with data already entered on each file—in essence, a mail merge feature. This prevents duplication of effort as alternatively, that information must be entered more than once into different programs and re-entered into documents needed for the representation.

Customer Relationship Management (CRM)/Sales Software

What I've unfortunately found is that the creators of law firm practice management software aren't marketers. I guess too many of them are former lawyers. They must know that the plaintiffs' firms they're providing software to need to market their services to bring in business, but the tools they provide are insufficient for that purpose; they're geared primarily for handling the tasks that happen only after a prospect becomes a client.

To do proper advanced marketing and intake department work, you'll need more than one software program—

one for the front end and one for the back end (though it's really the middle because you need another program for accounting, the real back end).

I once explained this to a law firm software consultant. He asked me what you might be asking right now: "Why in the world do you need another program? Can't you just use the case management software?" No. Here are the kinds of things you need to be able to do to have a competent marketing and intake system:

- automatically capture the information a prospect enters into your website without having to enter it manually and schedule the next action
- manually capture the contact information of every prospect who calls your office (except the ones who clearly don't qualify)
- track the lead source for each prospect to determine which marketing channels are delivering you leads
- trigger an automated multi-media follow-up campaign for all prospects until they become clients
- automatically send out your template follow-up emails (and even voice mails and text messages) that automatically merge with the data already in the program to personalize and customize them
- prompt someone in the office to make the appropriate phone call at the appropriate time in the follow-up campaign sequence or to attend, schedule, or remind a prospect about an appointment

- allow you to segment your list with tags or opportunities so you can direct the right message to the right person to avoid blasting the same generic message to your entire list
- prompt someone in your office or a third-party to send the appropriate mail piece to a list of people at a certain stage in the follow-up sequence, attaching the list in Excel to be merged with the attached document(s)
- allow you to run reports on key metrics important to your firm such as new leads, appointments, new cases, conversion rates, cost per lead, ROI, etc., and identify what's working and what isn't ideally on a simple summary report

Those are ideally what you want from your software program to help you manage this whole process. Many programs out there can do even more than this such as have shopping cart software built in and other advanced features (more on using CRM software in a later chapter).

Scanners: Going Paper-Less, Not Paperless

I learned a long time ago that a law firm cannot really be paperless; the entire business depends on what we do on and with paper. But a law firm can easily get by with less paper than most currently use and boost its efficiency in the process. This is what I mean by paper-less.

Think of all these time killers:

- creating files
- looking for files
- filing papers in the file
- hiring interns or low-pay clerks or overpaying high-priced people to file the papers and the files
- filing the files
- closing the files
- boxing up the files
- buying file cabinets
- needing more and more space for the files and cabinets
- paying to shred the files

We set out many years ago on this paper-less path and have never looked back. We scan all our new files and all our mail whether incoming or outgoing. Our scanners run optical character recognition (OCR) on all the text so we can use search tools to find the scanned document whether by title or individual words in the document. This allows our staff to search for and find the information they need on any file from any computer, iPhone, or iPad anywhere; they no longer need the file itself! If they're going to court and want something on paper, they simply print it, take it, and when they're done, they shred it. The only exception we make to this is very large discovery responses that come in on paper.

We simply keep them in files until the case is over and then scan them in and shred them.

All our checks, bills, bank statements, and deposits are scanned and shredded. We don't keep boxes of these documents anymore because we have electronic copies; we just don't have a need for originals.

We use the large scanner for big jobs such as the daily incoming and outgoing mail. Many staff members as well as the bookkeeper have small desktop scanners for quick jobs that come up throughout the day.

Another good reason for having a scanner is that it will allow you to convert a document into a format you can email, saving more time and money on paper, ink, and postage.

Templates

In most volume plaintiff law practices, dozens and dozens of documents are used repeatedly for all kinds of reasons. Yes, there may be a few variations of the same document depending on the facts, but beyond that, it's the same thing every time.

You should be creating a master template folder of all these documents. I don't care if it's the cover letter you use when you send a settlement check, the motions you use, the complaint, the thank-you letter, or your close-file letter. The list of such communications that can rely on a template is endless; no one should have to hunt around for a good one to use or God forbid reinvent the wheel every time one of these is needed!

You need to systematically find the best of all these documents, make final edits, and bless them as your firm's templates to be used by everyone with no or just minor variations. Put them in one place so everyone can access them. Templates get changed only with your approval. These are part of your systems and best practices, and you want everyone not only following your system but also using your templates. Otherwise, you won't have a consistent product and cannot grow.

Hot Docs

Hot Docs takes templates to a higher level. This software lets you fill out an interview form with all the facts about your client's case, and then it imports it into the templates you've set up. It can not only merge with a template; it can also pick the proper paragraphs based on the logic you've created in your questionnaire and assemble them into the perfect finished document. It will also change all the pronouns and plurals based on the gender of your client and whether there are multiple clients or just one. Depending on what type of law you practice, this can be a huge time saver, and it can even save you from costly errors of omission that can occur if you use the old-fashioned, cut-and-paste method of creating documents from different templates.

Auto-Fill Emails

An advanced strategy we started using was utilizing templates in emails. As we tried to cut costs and save time, we moved many of our communications from paper to email. So we created templates that auto-populated in our email body with the click of a button. We have a list of all the different templates in a drop-down menu in Outlook. When one of them is selected, the email populates with one of those templates! These require someone with basic programming skills to implement in Outlook.

Accounting Software

If you're running your firm using software for marketing, intake, and case management, you should have accounting software for all those same reasons. The benefits are tremendous, and the downside is almost nil.

Tracking Numbers

You can buy phone numbers to put in all your marketing materials that track where your calls are coming from, record the calls, and provide the contact information for the callers. You can find out how long the calls lasted, if they were answered, or if the caller hung up.

These are a great way to see which ads are making your phones ring and how your staff is handling callers. An unexpected benefit of these numbers is that once your staff knows they're being recorded, they'll behave better with the callers even when you're not around and even if you don't listen to the recordings that frequently!

Screen-Capture Software

This is free or inexpensive software that lets you quickly take a picture of all or part of what's on your screen, lets you write on that image if you want, and email it to someone. If your staff is having a problem or getting an error message, they can take a picture of it and email it to you or your IT person. Or let's say you're working on a website and want to show your designer what you want done. You can take a picture of it, draw arrows, add explanatory text, and fire it off.

This software also allows you to take a video of what's on your screen and captures your voice at the same time. So you can turn it on and go through the steps of how to open a new file on your software; it will capture all your keystroke and mouse movements while you explain what you're doing. Now you have a video on how to open a new file for your procedures library, so no one ever needs to explain the process to new staff members again. Once they have the link to the video, they can train themselves!

Evernote

This is a free tool that allows you to save notes, pictures, webpages, etc., but also tag them so you can find them later using a simple search box. Let's say you come across a great article, picture, or website you want to save. Before Evernote, you'd bookmark it, but after a couple of years, your bookmark list would be so long that it would be useless. You'd have to click on them all to find that site you saved because they're not searchable. And if you get a new computer, you usually lost all your bookmarks on the old computer.

With Evernote, you add a note or a tag about why you liked the page, article, or whatever before you save it. Two years down the road, you can locate that great picture of the Grand Canyon by typing in "grand canyon" and bingo—it pops up along with whatever notes you made about it.

Screen Sharing

This technology has come a long way to the point that you can now find free screen-sharing software. The idea behind this is that you can be on the phone with someone and share your screen with that person so he or she can see exactly what you're seeing. This is great for meetings and for working with technical support people to help you fix something. These come with other useful bells and whistles such as screen capture and video/audio recording of a session.

Remote Log-In

Imagine you're at home when you realize you forgot to bring home a document you need to finish before the morning. Years ago, you would have to get back in your car and drive back to the office to retrieve it. Depending on how far you live from your office, this could be a serious inconvenience and time waster. But with remote log-in software, you can now connect directly to your computer from your home or wherever and work as though you were actually sitting in your office. You have access to everything you would have if you were there, even the ability to hear the sound from that computer on your home computer. This also allows your staff or attorneys to be able to work from home at night or as telecommuters or your part-time bookkeeper to work remotely. Unless all your data and software is in the cloud, this type of software is simply a must have. This is another great reason to be paper-less.

Document Management Software

With a document management system, you can catalog documents in ways that make them accessible exactly when and where they're needed. With everyone following the same consistent, enforced rules, crucial documents that were previously lost or hard to find will be instantly available just when they are needed.

Document management typically gives organizations far more control over document security and access.

Confidential documents can be made available only to the people who need to see them.

Many document management systems also make it easy to set up boilerplate libraries for storing commonly used forms, templates, and basic documents—another major timesaver.

Desktop Faxing or Efaxing

Desktop faxing allows you to send and receive faxes from your computer through your email. This cuts down on costs by eliminating the need for paper, toner, and a fax line, and there is no equipment to buy, fix, and replace. This also eliminates the need to scan in the paper received from a fax, so you can be paper-less because it's already in electronic format. It also eliminates the need to put faxes in people's mailboxes or bins as you can have someone simply forward the emailed fax. If you have a piece of paper that needs to be faxed, you simply scan it in and fax it from your desktop.

Shredder

You should have a shredder for sensitive documents; they come in countless shapes, sizes, capacities, and prices. They all essentially do the same thing, but many can even shred staples and other items so no one has to spend time preparing your shred project before shredding.

Phone System

Whether you use an onsite phone system or virtual or hosted/cloud-based phone system, you need to have something that you can program quickly and relatively painlessly. This is because as you get more sophisticated, you'll want your phone system to route new callers a certain way, existing clients a certain way, and so on. You might want certain people to receive certain calls only or be in the first wave of responders to certain calls. You'll want one thing to happen during the day and another at night. You might want to add special mailboxes that serve the purpose of a free, recorded message. You'll probably end up wanting to move phones off-site to allow key employees to work from home, and you might want that for your own home office. You'll want these phones to connect to the network and work as if they were in the office.

You might want messages emailed instead of saved to a physical phone and even transcribed automatically as well as the audio file. (This feature is a great way to be able to forward messages to the proper person with instructions attached.) All these functions and more are available today for very little cost.

Shared/Public Folders

As you move to a more online and paper-less environment, you'll start using email more and more. And there are many items you will want multiple people to have access to. This can raise some questions: "How can I give access to emails Jane is getting to Jim but not give out Jane's personal email inbox to other people?" "How can I segregate just these types of emails from all the other emails Jane gets so there's no confusion and nothing slips through the cracks?"

We've found a great solution: public or shared folders in Microsoft Outlook (which may exist in other email programs; we just happen to use Outlook). These are email folders that have specific email addresses but are shared by more than one person. For example, you can direct all your incoming faxes to an email address such as faxes@yourlawfirm.com. They will all go to a folder in Outlook you label "faxes." You assign someone to check this folder throughout the day and forward faxes to the person named as the recipient and mark them in the folder with a check or something indicating they've been handled.

You can also give access to this folder to a backup person and yourself or your whole firm. However, this solves all the problems noted above as all the faxes are segregated; no one is sharing his or her personal inbox, multiple people have access, and you have a system for knowing when and how faxes have been handled.

Shared Drive for Files

Another resource you must have is some type of shared drive for all your files that everyone can access.

This can be done through a server in your office or through a cloud provider such as Google or Dropbox. This is the place where all your clients' files your office is working on will be kept. You may also have a folder for other shared documents such as your templates, policies and procedures documents, office forms, etc.

Adobe Acrobat Standard or Its Equivalent

Just about everyone is using Adobe in one form or another. According to Wikipedia, "In 1993, Adobe introduced PDF, the Portable Document Format, and its Adobe Acrobat and Reader software. PDF is now an International Standard and is adopted worldwide as a common medium for electronic documents." Adobe accomplished this by giving the software away for free. However, the free version is missing some important elements that law firm and companies trying to go paper-less must have.

First is optical character recognition, OCR, which I mentioned earlier. It is a technology that enables you to convert scanned paper documents into editable and searchable data. This allows you to more easily and quickly find saved PDF documents using any search tool by not only the name of the document but also by any of the words in the document itself!

A second vitally important feature is the ability to chop up or combine documents. For example, assume you have a pile of papers scanned and emailed to you and you don't want all of them saved with the same filename. You can simply select the pages you want removed and create a new PDF out of just those pages and save it while keeping intact the source file either as it was originally or without the pages you've removed. Similarly, you can combine PDF files into one file or even change the order of the pages.

A third function I've found very useful is the typewriter tool in Adobe. With this tool, you can take a form that has been emailed to you to fill out and literally type in your answers as if you were running it through an old-fashioned typewriter. You don't need a typewriter, and you don't have to print it out and hand-write in your answers.

There are probably dozens more features in the full-blown version of Adobe that are useful in one way or another but are beyond the scope of this book. The bottom line is that every law firm must have it or its equivalent.

Microsoft Office—Word and Excel

I would image every law firm has had experience with Microsoft Word or its equivalent. Obviously, law firms are in the document creation business, and you cannot create documents without word processing software of some kind. Therefore, I will not spend much time on Microsoft Word. However, there is another very useful program that a lot of lawyers are not very skilled at that comes with Microsoft Office, and that is Excel.

While most lawyers and staff members do not have much use for Excel, if you are the owner or a partner in a law firm, you should learn how to use some of the key functions of Excel. It will significantly increase your ability to accurately analyze and manipulate key metrics in your firm. And you will be able to more quickly create your own reports or manipulate reports given to you by others without waiting for them to do it and get it back to you. Make it a rule that any report sent to you be sent in Excel, not PDF, for this very reason.

I won't go into a tutorial on Excel in this book, as many of these functions are very easy to look up online these days. I will just mention some of the ones you should be aware of and should try to master. You should be able to:

- create formulas to apply to rows and rows of data to allow you to add, subtract, average, show days elapsed, ROI, percentages, etc.
- be able to quickly drag a formula to other cells so that it updates itself or repeats itself across rows of data
- be able to drag one or more cells to different areas of the spreadsheet to quickly move things from one location to another without having to retype it all
- insert, delete, and show or hide comments and make other changes to the size, color, and location of data in a cell
- wrap data so it remains inside its cell and doesn't run over the edges or unwrap data
- merge and unmerge cells

- hide columns and rows of data
- resize one or more columns or rows to fit the data in the cells with a couple clicks
- create and use multiple tabs in one Excel document and connect them with formulas
- duplicate a spreadsheet in another tab or create a new blank one
- split a column of data into two columns, such as an address into the number in one column and the street name into another with a few clicks
- sort rows or columns by smallest to largest or A to Z, etc.
- change data in a cell or rows of cells into text, date, number, dollars, etc.
- create graphs based on data

Finally, I should mention that all your data should be backed up in more than one place. If you have computers or servers with data on them, you must get an external backup of some kind in case they fail. This could be cloud-based or physical disks. If you have your firm's data in the cloud, you may want to investigate whether a copy is being saved locally to your computer/server or whether it's possible to make that happen. As we have all seen, even the biggest companies can fail, and you don't want to be at anyone's mercy with your most important asset—your database(s)!

And don't forget to have your IT help run test restores from this backup database every so often to ensure it will actually work in case of an emergency.

CHAPTER 11

It's All about Who

Trading Time for Money: The Lawyer's Self-Limiting Business Model

Okay, so you've overcome your mind-set issues. It's time to take your business to the next level and make the money you feel you deserve and always wanted. But there's another big problem. As a professional, a lawyer, your income is limited by the number of hours you have in a day. So, what do most lawyers do to earn more money? You guessed it. They work more hours. As we all know, that's a recipe for an unhappy life, unhappy family, and burnout. Maybe even alcoholism or drug abuse.

On top of that, the longer you work, the less you make per hour. Remember those students in law school who were offered big salaries by the big law firms? It all sounded so glamorous at the time; I was envious of the money they were going to make. But I later realized that in many cases, I was making more than they were per hour, and I had a life on top of my job. For example, if you earn $80,000 but have to put in eighty hours a week to earn it, you're earning $20 an hour. On the other hand, if you're earning $50,000 but working only forty hours a week, you're actually earning $25 an hour. I was making more per hour, and my extra hours allowed me to have a life.

The other problem with this business model is that if you're away from your office, you're not making any money, right? So what you really have instead of a business is a job. If you don't do your job, you don't make any money. The good news is there's a way around this for most plaintiffs' lawyers. You can earn more money and still have a life if you learn how to leverage yourself. You have to be paid for more than just your time. The first way to do that is to … Yes! Hire another lawyer to do what you do.

Here comes another mind-set shift. This requires you to give up the limelight. You have to be able to let your attorney(s) get some or all of the credit for a job well done. You also have to set up your practice so people are either not coming to the firm primarily to hire you, or if they are, you're playing the role of overseer, not laborer. This way, you're involved but in a leveraged fashion, and that will begin to sever the time-for-money link and result in growth.

Dan Kennedy says that the secret that causes the biggest leaps for many small business owners, professional practices, and entrepreneurs is a mind-set shift (here's another one); they stop looking at themselves as the chief doers of whatever it is that makes them money and become the chief marketers of whatever it is that makes them money. You could be the best lawyer in the world, but if you're not getting the word out every day and to the right audience, you'll never have the number of clients you desire.

I'm sure you know or know of many lawyers in your market you consider average lawyers but nonetheless have thriving practices due to their marketing. They've shifted from focusing on being the best lawyers to being the best marketers. Due to the bar association's rules restricting comparisons and other restrictions, the public is left with very little to go on to distinguish between lawyers other than their marketing. And if you have a real niche practice, your potential clients won't know you exist if you don't employ effective marketing.

But to bring on another attorney, you need to have what? Right—more cases. To get more cases, you'll have to do better and more marketing. We'll deal with marketing in a later chapter, but here, let me say that if you're thinking about hiring an attorney, it can become the chicken or the egg problem, a Catch-22. If you start by getting more cases first, you'll need another attorney to help handle them. On the other hand, if you get the attorney first, what will he or she do until your caseload builds? And how will you pay that attorney until then? Next are some ideas to help solve this.

CHAPTER 12

Hiring Your First Attorney

First, you must know that you can actually get more business for a new associate before you hire one. It would not be very fair to your new attorney to quit his or her job, come aboard your firm, and then find out in a few months that you're unable to create enough work to keep him or her employed. So you have to begin with the marketing and the proof that you can create enough new business to justify hiring another attorney. And you must be sure you can create it on an ongoing basis for at least the foreseeable future.

To help with the overload, you could associate with an attorney on an "of counsel" basis and just feed that attorney the overflow work as you perfect your marketing. Once you're getting enough cases that can support a full-time associate, you hire the associate and end the of-counsel relationship. Or you could take on the extra cases with your current staff knowing that when the pressure builds to the point you're about to burst, you will relieve it with the new person. The last thing you want to do is bring on an expensive new attorney and spend months paying him or her to perform at half capacity.

Your next question may be, "Yes, Craig, I think we can manage to hire an associate, but my current staff is maxed out, and I can't hire an associate and more staff. It's just too much money!" The answer is what we called the chief cook and bottle washer. Most attorneys who join small law firms aren't expecting blue-chip law firm treatment. If they are, believe me, they're the wrong lawyers to hire and won't last long. You can simply explain during the interview that you're hiring your first attorney for a ground-floor opportunity. As such, you expect the new attorney to do everything on his or her cases with no staff. As your caseload grows and more revenue comes in, that's when you hire staff so your new attorney can leverage himself or herself (exactly as you're doing by employing that attorney). Your attorney's job will start out just like yours was when you started as a solo practitioner. You did everything in the beginning, and so will your new attorney!

When you make this move, you might find yourself taking one step back before you can take two steps forward. In figure 4 on the following page, you'll see how you will typically dig a small hole while the new attorney is paying for himself or herself, but it should return to break even and then profitability shortly thereafter if you have hired the right person and you have the right amount of work for him or her to handle. You can see that the cumulative loss is at its largest in month 4—approximately $20,000. Thereafter, net income is positive and the cumulative loss continues to diminish as the months of positive net income accumulate.

	Month	1	2	3	4	5	6	7	8
Settlements		0	2	3	5	6	7	9	12
Avg Fee/Fees	2,100	0	4,200	6,300	10,500	12,600	14,700	18,900	25,200
Collected Fees				2,100	5,200	8,400	11,550	13,650	16,800
Salary	50,000	4,875	4,875	4,875	4,875	4,167	4,167	4,167	4,167
Incentive	8%	0	0	168	420	672	924	1,092	1,344
	Total Comp	4,875	4,875	5,043	5,295	4,839	5,091	5,259	5,511
Ad Expense		4,500	4,500	4,500	4,500	4,500	4,500	4,500	4,500
Add'l Staff	30,000				2,500	2,500	2,500	2,500	2,500
	Net Income	-9,375	-5,175	-3,243	-1,795	761	2,609	6,641	12,689
	Cumulative	-9,375	-14,550	-17,793	-19,588	-18,827	-16,217	-9,576	3,113

Figure 4: Financial Impact and Catch-Up Period for New Attorney

Keep in mind that this could happen more than once as you build your firm, and you might have to take less pay for a time to help make ends meet. But consider these sacrifices as investments in your future, parts of a plan that will come to fruition and ultimately work to your greatest benefit.

CHAPTER 13

Who Is on Your Bus and What Seat Are They In?

Once I had my systems in place, I believed I could hire just about anyone to do the attorney job and he or she would succeed. Boy, was I wrong. After hiring and training dozens of lawyers over the years, I agree with the findings of Jim Collins in his book *Good to Great* that having the right people on your bus is critical for your success.

You have to determine exactly what it takes for someone you hire to succeed in the position for which you're hiring. Attorneys aren't all created equal. Some are very good at research and writing but have no personality or sales ability and shouldn't go anywhere near a potential new client, a negotiation, or a trial. Others are great talkers and negotiators but are no good at research and writing or simply don't like it. Some have strong beliefs about how things should be done in a law firm, while others are malleable and will follow the system without constantly questioning it. The list goes on ...

Over the years, we have learned through our mistakes all the areas to probe in potential new attorneys to determine whether they are a good fit for what we do and our firm. To really drill down on their beliefs, we even have questions we have them answer in writing as part of the interview process that have no right or wrong answers, but they give us insight as to how they will think about the myriad important issues that surround handling clients and cases once they come aboard our firm. We want good philosophical "matches" working for us.

The truth is that when you hire the right people, they will find a way to pay for themselves and make your life easier and make you money. They will take their jobs seriously and treat your business as their own. They will go the extra mile. They will invest in the job emotionally as well as physically. You'll get their brains as well as their bodies.

You also want to make sure you hire correctly because of the problem caused by the weak link. When you have a weak link on your team, everyone else has to do more to cover for that person. That will hold you back from attaining your goals—having a business that can run itself without you being present and achieving peak profitability.

CHAPTER 14

Hire Slow, Fire Fast

You've probably heard the saying "Hire slow, fire fast." There's much truth in it, but I think most law firms find it hard to follow. First, if you're busy and a member of your staff gives you two weeks' notice, there is huge internal pressure to find someone who can quickly get up to speed with the work that was left behind. It can take at least a week just to get the first person in for an interview. If you wanted to spend a month combing through candidates and then another month interviewing a number of candidates and putting them through some hoops, your staff would be squealing and you could find yourself having to do things personally you'd rather not.

On the other hand, it's eerie how often the best candidate for the job is one of the first if not the first to apply. I find it's usually very easy to narrow down the field to two or three candidates after the first in-person interviews (or even after a phone interview and then one in-person interview). At that point, you can have them do any tests you want, check references, and have them interview with anyone from your team, even you again. This final phase shouldn't take an inordinate amount of time. But if you skip steps in the process and try to hire quickly, you'll often end up with a bad hire who will cost you even more time and expense to unwind and start the process over.

Over the years, my fire-fast muscle has been strengthened. In the early years, I had a belief that if I continued to work with someone, I could somehow transform him or her into at least an average if not a perfect employee. But what I found over time was that people are who they are. Some don't care or are just incapable of doing the job they were hired to do (or they were able to do the job for someone else but for some reason won't or can't do the job for you).

These are very uncomfortable situations; most of us don't like to fire people. However, those who aren't doing their jobs well usually know that. Many times, they aren't happy with the situation either, but they are afraid to make the first move. The longer they stay in your firm, the more damage they'll do and the more frustration they'll cause you and your staff. Someone will inevitably be either covering for them or be affected by their mistakes. If they aren't giving their best efforts and you leave them there, your staff will be thinking, *Why am I working so hard if that person can get away with dogging it?*

By letting unsatisfactory employees go, you're freeing them up to find their place in the world. Just because they aren't working out for you doesn't mean they won't flourish elsewhere. The longer you keep them on, the longer it will take them to find this place where they can be much happier.

I remember this situation clearly with one staff member we hired to handle all the settlements. We created a new position, pulled all this work off our litigation paralegals, and created a settlement paralegal position. We had a system for him to follow that involved a certain number of calls and emails at certain predetermined times. It was all computerized; all he had to do was follow the system. The system ensured that nothing would fall through the cracks whether on the defendant's end, our end, or the client's end.

After this person started, the number of checks we were receiving seemed to slow down, and before long, we were having some cash-flow issues. Our accounts receivable report showed the number of checks dragging out beyond ninety days kept growing and growing. Here, reports came in handy (more on these later). So I began to have regular meetings with this paralegal to find out what was happening with all the old settlements. At those meetings, I would hear one of three things: 1. He had followed the system, but the clients were not responding or the defendants were dragging their feet; 2. The attorneys had done something during the settlement discussions to anger the clients causing them to be unresponsive; or 3. Don't worry, "the check is in the mail!"

Walking by his desk periodically, I sensed that this staff person was on the phone only when it was time to gossip but never doing the follow up prescribed by our system. My head paralegal and some other team members echoed my observation in private.

But I asked myself, *Who will handle these settlements if I make a change? What if I'm wrong? This will be a lot of work. Our cash-flow issues could get worse, not better. Then what?* I came up with countless fear-based excuses not to do anything drastic. I ended up letting this situation go on far too long, and it caused me to waste dozens of hours with him. It frustrated not only me but also my team and all our clients whose checks were delayed.

I don't recall the final straw, but I finally summoned enough guts to make a change. We found a fantastic candidate. I'm sure you can guess what happened next. Yes, it was nirvana. After I put the right person in the right seat on our bus, as Jim Collins would say, everything went back to the way it was supposed to be. She picked up on the system quickly and followed it properly. Checks came in regularly and on time. I never had to meet with her to check on things. Clients were happy, the staff was happy, and so was I. She even improved the system, and before long, she was in line to be promoted to a litigation paralegal.

I kicked myself for not having made the change months earlier. I'd known something was wrong from the beginning, but I let it fester hoping I could coach this person to success. Once again, had I not let fear dictate my decision, had I fired fast, we all would have been far better off.

CHAPTER 15

What's Their Highest and Best Use?

I'll never forget one of the emails I received from a departing team member when we were at the height of our expansion. As we grew, we did what any litigation firm would do. We added attorneys to do the legal work—negotiations, prepare motions, sign documents, go to court, etc. To help them, we added paralegals who handled all the correspondence, legal documents, filing, copying, mailing, and scheduling for pre- and post-suit activities. However, as we have discussed, we had a template for virtually every routine document that could arise in one of our cases. Most of the time, the paralegal only had to find the information from the intake document, plug it into the proper template, and send it or perform a merge function from our software program.

Well, this particular paralegal complained that the job was beneath her and wasn't really a paralegal job at all. After I read that, I got to thinking about how I could better match our jobs to the talent level of the paralegal being hired to avoid this job dissatisfaction and reduce turnover. And bingo, it hit me! Not only was I able to solve the dissatisfaction problem, but at the same time, I found a way to save us literally tens of thousands of dollars per month (we had a pretty large group of paralegals).

We made sure each person was working at his or her highest and best use. We did this by pushing lower-level tasks down to the lowest-level person who could competently handle them. First, we broke up the litigation paralegal job into two jobs. This was the creation of a new job we called the junior paralegal position. This included all the pre-suit activity such as:

- preparing demand letters
- preparing informal arbitration letters
- gathering paperwork missing from the file
- organizing the file and preparing fact summary sheets
- scheduling pre-suit activity
- preparing the Complaint
- preparing and stuffing envelopes, adding postage, etc. to get the mail out
- making copies as needed
- filing loose documents in the proper file (we weren't paper-less yet)

This was an entry-level job in the legal field; it allowed us to basically create a farm system for our litigation paralegal position, which was more challenging and required more skill. It also created an opportunity for advancement; those in this junior position had something to work toward.

The litigation paralegal kept all the post-suit activity such as:

- ensuring Answers were filed and court dates were set property in the software
- keeping the attorney's litigation calendar
- talking to clients about their answers to Discovery and preparing Answers
- preparing routine Briefs, Motions, and Summaries
- performing research
- outlining depositions, organizing exhibits, and preparing trial notebooks
- talking to defense counsel, the court, and clients as needed
- handling releases and checks and any other post-suit matters that arose

Because they weren't handling tasks they were overqualified for and that they felt were beneath them, they were working at their highest and best use. They had become manager level and had assistants. Everyone felt challenged and was happier, creating less turnover and we had created entry-level jobs with real opportunity for advancement!

Even better, it created the following cost savings. Let's say your litigation paralegal gets paid $35,000. If you need four litigation paralegals to function in your office, you're spending $140,000. Add approximately 10 percent for payroll taxes, worker's compensation, etc., and you're at ***$154,000***. Now let's assume you can take two of those litigation paralegals and create two junior paralegal positions out of them. You can decide exactly what those positions should pay, but let's say something under $30,000. I think we paid around $25,000 for those positions.

So the new financial picture is this: two litigation paralegals at $35,000 each = $70,000. Two junior paralegal positions at $25,000 each = $50,000. The new total for all four is $120,000 plus 10 percent = ***$132,000***. So your savings are ***$154,000 - $132,000*** = $22,000 per year! Over the next five years, that is an additional $110,000! Additionally, in some firms, the litigation paralegal gets an office. I would argue that junior paralegals are more akin to legal secretaries, and so they are usually not found in an office. Therefore, you can save the office cost as well and put them in a cubicle or at a desk in front of the offices.

You will find other opportunities to do the same thing with different functions as you grow. For example, the next task that all the junior paralegals were doing that could be pushed down to an even lower level was the mail. At one point, we had approximately six junior paralegal positions. A big part of their work each day was to print out documents, get them signed, copy them, prepare the envelopes, put postage on the envelopes, and mail them. This part of the job does not take any legal skill whatsoever and can be done by a "mail clerk" at $8 to $10 per hour. Don't forget that to have a junior paralegal do this costs approximately $13 per hour. So a full-time mail clerk would cost approximately $20,000 annually plus taxes and benefits. Your junior paralegal costs approximately $25,000 per year plus taxes and benefits. By doing this, we were able to eliminate one or more of our junior paralegals, and those who remained were happier because they now had their own assistants and were eliminating work they didn't want to do! And for many firms, it's likely that when you give all the mail work to the mail clerk, it won't be a full-time position, so the savings are even greater.

The other opportunity this creates is if you are in growth mode, you are able to handle more cases/clients without having to hire any more skilled paralegals. Each time the work starts to bubble over and the complaints come that they cannot keep up, you can simply pull lower-level tasks off them and hire less-expensive help to do them. So, your first move is to hire a junior paralegal instead of another litigation paralegal and give him or her all the lower-level work from the litigation paralegals. Then at the next stage of growth, you hire the mail clerk to push yet again more work down from the junior paralegal, freeing the junior paralegal up to take on more work from the paralegals. In our firm, we found tasks such as mail, processing settlements, and scheduling were ripe for this strategy. Now you have solved the growth problem, made people happier, and saved money!

You may hear from your staff that this won't work, so you'll have to sell them on the idea. They need to see how great it will be for them to get rid of unchallenging work, handle more-challenging tasks, and possibly earn a promotion. You need to let them know you want them working at their highest and best use for everyone's benefit.

If they're valued for their litigation skills, they shouldn't be wasting their time making copies and so on. Many won't buy in completely until they see it in action and working. But it does work.

CHAPTER 16

Keeping Them Happy: How to Design Incentives for Maximum Productivity

Okay, so your staff is happy now, but what about your attorneys? One of the most important things you can do for your attorneys is provide them with a monetary incentive. I'm a big believer in incentives, especially for attorneys. I can still remember early on when I was sharing space with another law firm. One of my friends was an attorney at this personal injury firm. He had a very large docket because his firm did a lot of advertising, and he was being paid reasonably well.

One day, he told me about a six-figure settlement he had made for the firm. I asked him if he had received anything extra for that, and he told me no. I asked him whether he would see a larger end-of-year bonus, and he bemoaned the small bonus he had received the year before and expected that nothing would change for that year. It was out of his control; he was expecting to be disappointed.

Now what do you think his motivation level will be to maximize the recovery on any given case on his docket? We all know that attorneys play a substantial counseling role with their clients in terms of what the ultimate settlement looks like. They can strongly recommend a settlement in one instance where more-motivated attorneys will strongly discourage a settlement because they know that if they push harder and longer, they will likely get additional compensation from the defendant. So you as a business owner will be spending money to bring in cases to hand to someone who is simply not aligned with your expectation that he or she will maximize the value of the cases that attorney is asked to handle.

Now let's assume that you tell attorneys in the interview process that they will be paid a fair base pay plus performance-based compensation (PBC) they can exert control over. You set up a plan by which they will receive a certain percentage (e.g., 5 to 10 percent) of every dollar in net attorney's fees (excluding costs) the firm receives from the docket of cases they are responsible for.

I try to design the plan so that their base pay is a little below the market; so my attorneys are not completely comfortable coasting on their base pay alone. But when their base pay is combined with the PBC, they can substantially exceed market compensation and be at the high end of the pay scale. This completely aligns your attorneys' financial interests with yours, the owner of the firm. The more money you make, the more money they make. You set this up in a way that makes good economic sense for all parties.

I find it helpful to show them graphically with a spreadsheet how much they can expect to earn using assumptions from your firm's past performance. You can show them below-average, average, and above-average models with corresponding PBC totals.

Do you think if you hire the right people that they might do a better job for you than those who are in the dark about their end-of-year compensation? Do you think they might stick around your firm longer than those who are constantly complaining or frustrated by their discretionary bonuses? Do you think you would attract better talent with this type of compensation structure (all else being equal) than the alternative? And what if you made these payments monthly or quarterly instead of waiting until the end of the year—might that also help?

I argue yes to all the above. Although your employees will always be in positions fundamentally different from yours as their employer and have divergent interests as a result, the closer you can align your and their interests, the better off your firm will be.

You can also provide a financial incentive for your staff. Here comes another possible mind-set shift. You may think that this somehow runs afoul of the rules on splitting fees with nonlawyers, but the truth is that you are not basing this on the amount of the fees earned. This is a performance-based incentive, no different from paying your staff bonuses at the end of the year based on some type of performance standard you have designed.

Look at what areas of your firm are the key drivers of performance or what areas are the bottlenecks holding back your firm from achieving optimal performance. I have used this with the people responsible for the intake process to make sure we are following up with everyone on a timely basis and doing everything we can to ensure we reach our new case goals.

Another example might be filing bankruptcy petitions. Perhaps your staff needs an extra incentive to ensure you file X petitions per month or file X complaints per month. Or maybe you are doing a bad job collecting checks and your receivables are way behind. You could incentivize someone to collect X checks per month. This is an area in which you can get creative, so look around and experiment with some different ideas and, yes, even have some fun with it!

CHAPTER 17

Tips on Delegating Tasks

The way our firm delegates tasks involves documenting the steps involved in each task whether using a video of what we're doing on the computer or a written document with screen shots. This is easy using one of the software tools we discussed in an earlier chapter. We go over the training with those who will be responsible for the tasks. After feeling that they have been trained, we continue to check carefully that they are doing each step correctly. Once we find that there doesn't appear to be any regular errors occurring and all steps are happening as designed, we spot-check every so often and don't inspect as rigidly. Eventually, when the spot-checking seems futile, that ends as well.

You must think short term and long term when doing these training videos/manuals. You will be tempted not to take the time to do this. In the short term, you are creating the documentation needed to train new personnel to help your business grow and free up your time. In the long term, you are creating the manuals and systems that will allow anyone new to learn how to do this job with minimal time invested by a trainer, especially you. This will also slowly build up your library of policies and procedures manuals and videos, which will make your firm more valuable.

CHAPTER 18

Steering the Ship

How to Manage Chaos in the Least Amount of Time

There is a saying in business that there's what you want to happen, there's what you think is happening, and there's what is actually happening. Most law firm owners are absolutely convinced they know what is actually happening in their offices. When things are not going the way they expect, they refuse to believe it may be one or more of their longtime, trusted staff members causing the problem. So how do you figure out what's happening when things aren't going the way you want? The answer starts with managing by the numbers.

In the early years of my firm, I had no clue how important it was to know my numbers. When things are going well and you're growing, it may seem unnecessary, but I can tell you from experience, this is necessary even when you're making money. What happened with us was that the only number I was paying attention to was the number of active cases in our case-management software. If it looked okay to me when I got around to checking it, I felt things were fine. If it started to drop, I would inquire about new cases further. But I was not following how many new cases we were retaining on a regular basis.

This was a very inaccurate way of keeping track because the number of active cases can be affected by more than one factor such as how many are settling, when they settle, and even how old they are and how fast they are being closed and moved off the list by your staff. It's like the horse with blinders on that can see only what's directly in front of it but cannot see the storm brewing behind it or to the side of it.

Over the course of many months, I saw our active cases dropping and not rebounding. In the past, I would see some ebb and flow and figured that was normal, but this time, things never returned to normal levels. When I looked deeper, I found that for many months in a row, our new cases were down significantly. I realized I was behind the eight ball because I was putting out a raging forest fire when I could have been dealing with a small brush fire had I caught it earlier.

In a volume-based plaintiff litigation firm, if the case flow changes, it's not too long before settlements change, revenue drops, and you can't afford your overhead.

The only way to properly steer the ship is to have a firm grasp of all the key performance indicators (KPI) in your business. A KPI is a business metric used to evaluate factors that are crucial to the success of a business. These should include what's happening at the front end of the business as well as the middle and the back ends of the business. Here is a list of KPIs and reports common to most plaintiffs' practices:

- leads generated from all marketing activities by source
- appointments generated from leads
- show rate for appointments set
- cases/clients generated from appointments
- successful cases/clients if contingency practice/ amount billed
- percentage of cases/clients who quit, fail, and/or are lost as well as billable time written off
- average fee per case/client
- percent of receivables collected
- average time to collect receivables
- profit and loss statements on both an accrual and cash basis
- cash-flow statement—checks in bank
- balance sheet

When you have attorneys working for you, you also want to run many of these reports based on the individual attorneys so you can uncover differences in performance. If you have never done this, you will likely be astonished at what you find.

Let's look at each of these reports and what they can reveal to you about your business. First, you need to know how many leads are being generated from all your marketing activities. This report will break down each marketing channel separately and show you how many leads are being produced by each. Leads counted should include all emails, texts, calls, forms filled out, voicemails, caller IDs, free reports requested—you get the idea. All those who have in one way or another raised their hands in response to your marketing should be captured here as leads no matter how cold you may deem those leads.

The second report depends on how you run your law firm, but most need to make an appointment as their next step with a prospect who calls for the first time. You need to know how many appointments you are setting for every lead produced by your marketing dollars.

And last, you need to know how many of those appointments are turning into new clients. If you have more than one attorney conducting these appointments, by all means run this report for each attorney. This will alert you to differences in performance that could be costing you thousands of dollars in lost opportunities.

So now you have a client, and depending on the type of practice you have, you need to monetize the relationship. This could be a contingency, a flat fee for a service, or old-fashioned billable time. You basically need to create reports around your particular practice area that show you how successful you and your attorneys have been in reaching your goals for the representation. How many settlements are you getting per week, month, and year? How many flat fees are you collecting? How much billable time are you billing and collecting? And so on.

Two things that can bite you in the butt if you're not paying attention to them are average fee and lost cases. If you have a contingency practice, it's easy to get caught up in the number of settlements you achieve per month, but if you're not watching your average fee, you could be losing thousands.

Once, we hired an attorney to help us with a new practice area during the 2009 recession. We had projections on how many cases we needed to settle per month, and they assumed an average fee based on what the firm had been receiving to date. The attorney was a very smart and experienced litigation attorney. He started very strong and hit the expected numbers very quickly. So after a couple months of this, I stopped checking the average fee and focused only on the total settlements. This went on for at least three months until I began to wonder why our cash flow wasn't stronger despite the fact we were continually hitting or getting close to our goals for settlements.

On our about month four, I took a deeper look at what was happening on the settlement report with total settlements and average fees *by attorney*. Lo and behold, I found that the new attorney was taking cheap settlements in order to boost his settlement totals and the average fee was off by around $800 per case! He was killing his ability to earn what he wanted in bonus money and was killing the firm's revenue even though he was getting many settlements and it appeared to him and us on the surface that he was doing a good job!

It is not uncommon to find that your attorneys will resolve difficult cases for less than you think they are worth; over time in this scenario, your average fee will slip. In our practice, a small change of only a couple hundred dollars can make a significant impact on our bottom line.

To illustrate the impact of this, let's assume a firm has 500 settlements per year. Simply multiply 500 settlements times $200 on average and you get $100,000! Or assume a $500 difference on 200 settlements and you get $100,000! Conversely, there may be opportunities to increase your average by focusing on it and improve your bottom line dramatically. Remember, this does not cost you anything in added personnel, equipment, marketing, or other expenses—it's pure profit!

The other thing to pay close attention to is how many of these cases are being closed or lost. It's easy to not pay attention to this when your practice gets to the point that you have other attorneys handling cases. When they can't reach a client, they will simply send a CYA letter and close the file. Or clients will call in and say they don't want to continue and they close the file. Or the case falls apart after further inquiry and fact gathering in their opinion. Or they lose on summary judgment or some other time during litigation. File closed. This can add up to a lot of files if you're not paying attention, and you'll be wondering why you cannot reach your goals despite seeing the proper number of new cases being signed up each month.

Last, you need to receive a few common financial statements at least once a month. This usually starts with an income statement or a profit and loss statement. Some P&Ls have so few lines that they show you just the tip of the iceberg, not what's happening beneath the surface. My opinion is that these statements should have categories set up for all your regular expenses with enough detail for you to see changes, spot issues, and correct them.

For example, instead of just having a line for marketing expenses, you can have subcategories for each type. That way, you will be able to see how much you are spending on online advertising, direct mail, radio, TV, etc. You can decide how much detail you want to see or not see; it's in part just personal preference.

Whether you set a budget for each expense at the beginning of the year or you just have some averages from the past year to base it on, you should know what your average month of expenses should be. Then you will know your break-even number and can quickly size up how you are doing based on the number of settlements or whatever other number in your firm represents a revenue-generating event.

Make sure you also see your profit and loss (P&L) statement on both an accrual and cash basis. These two reports give you a balanced view of how your practice is doing. The biggest problem with a cash-basis P&L is that you can choose whom to pay and when to pay; so the net income number is not accurate. Furthermore, when cash is collected, it is out of your control to a certain extent as well; you could have a real good or bad quarter due to variations in cash collected and which bills were paid. Whereas the accrual-based P&L tells you whether you were in fact profitable in a given period of time based on your actual case results or fees billed as well as the bills you owe regardless of whether you in fact paid them or not.

In most accounting programs, once all the data is entered, it's simply a click of a button as to whether you want to see the P&L on a cash or an accrual basis. We create a receivable when a case is settled for the amount of our fees and costs (as well as the client's portion) with the date of the settlement. This allows us to run the A/R report with the proper aging to be able to find settlements that are getting very old with no payment and perform some follow-up.

Next, you need some form of a cash-flow statement. I have found two useful ways to watch our cash flow over the years. Both of these are home-grown reports, not something I have found in QuickBooks. The first is a simple calculator that shows how much we have put in our general operating account as attorneys' fee deposits each banking day and extrapolates that to the total end of the month cash collected. This is then compared to our monthly cash collected target to give us a running picture at any point in the month of whether we are on track to hit our goal, exceed it, or fall short of it. So depending on how often you make deposits, you can have this report run daily, semiweekly, weekly, every two weeks, or bimonthly. These intervals are also dependent on how regular your cash collected is. If you have high-volume, small-average fees and/or high overhead expenses and unpredictable cash flow, you will want to run this report more often than if you have large-average fees and/or low overhead and regular and sufficient cash flow to cover your expenses. You can see an example of ours in figure 5 on the following page.

Day of Week	Day of Month	Banking Days	Daily Bank Deposit	Cumulative Total	Cumulative Avg	Projected Collections	Shortfall/ Overage
M	1	1	5,000	5,000	5,000	45,000	(15,000)
T	2						
W	3						
TH	4	2	6,000	11,000	5,500	49,500	(10,500)
F	5						
SA	6						
SU	7						
M	8	3	4,500	15,500	5,167	46,500	(13,500)
T	9						
W	10						
TH	11	4	6,500	22,000	5,500	49,500	(10,500)
F	12						
SA	13						
SU	14						
M	15	5	7,500	29,500	5,900	53,100	(6,900)
T	16						
W	17						
TH	18	6	7,000	36,500	6,083	54,750	(5,250)
F	19						
SA	20						
SU	21						
M	22	7	6,500	43,000	6,143	55,286	(4,714)
T	23						
W	24						
TH	25	8	9,000	52,000	6,500	58,500	(1,500)
F	26						
SA	27						
SU	28						
M	29	9	8,000	60,000	6,667	---	0
T	30						
W	31						

Monthly Goal	60,000
Total Banking Days	9
Avg Needed Per Banking	6,667

Figure 5: Running Total for Cash Collected Versus Goal

The other cash-flow report is a running export of our general ledger from our accounting program with an opening balance, a list of all credits and debits, and any pending deposits in our IOLTA account that will turn into fees collected in a matter of days. This allows me to see the current balance actually in the bank account as of the date the report is created. This can be different than the balance showing in your bank account because it may not reflect outstanding checks that have not been cashed or deposits that have not cleared. Then if cash is tight, you can simply add proposed payables below the balance line and, using a simple subtraction formula in Excel, determine which bills can be paid before you run out of money. You can see an example of ours in figure 6 on following page.

The cash-flow reports in our accounting program were unable to produce these exact reports and had bells and whistles that were not useful to us. We found that our books had to be set up and maintained a certain way for them to work. None of my bookkeepers could ever make the standard programs work for our business, so we just made our own.

You may be able to find a cash-flow report that works for you in your accounting program. It will likely not have the cash projected for the month versus your monthly goal, but it may provide you with an accurate picture of what is in your bank account at any given time. Many times, these reports take the check balance, add receivables and payables, and give you a net balance. However, if you only enter payables when you pay bills, this will throw off this report, among

	Date	Num	Name	Debit	Credit	Balance
10000 – XYZ Bank						44,739.27
10001 – Firm Accounts						44,739.27
10010 - Firm #xxxxxxx						30,774.27
	2/01/16		M Business Systems - Mita K4040		20.00	30,754.27
	2/01/16		Mega Internet		270.00	30,484.27
	2/01/16		COSE		350.00	30,134.27
	2/03/16		Deposit	24,949.17		55,083.44
	2/03/16		COSE/Medical Mutual		725.56	54,357.88
	2/04/16	23776	Hancock County Clerk of Courts - OH		350.00	54,007.88
	2/05/16		UPS		81.83	53,926.05
	2/05/16	23778	Athens County Clerk of Courts - OH		151.00	56,775.05
	2/08/16		XYZ Bookkeeping Services		1,750.00	52,0250.05
	2/10/16		A Technology Solutions, Inc.		772.74	51,252.31
	2/10/16		Business Source		53.84	51,198.47
	2/10/16		Total Census		511.68	50,686.76
	2/11/16	23779	Richland County Clerk of Courts		215.00	50,471.79
	2/11/16	23780	Seneca County Clerk of Courts - OH		300.00	50,171.79
	2/11/16	23781	Lake County Clerk of Courts - OH		190.00	49,981.79
	2/11/16	23782	Stark County Clerk of Courts - OH		523.00	49,458.79
	2/11/16	23783	Lorain County Clerk of Courts - OH		300.00	49,158.79
	2/11/16	23784	Lake County Clerk of Courts - OH		190.00	48,968.79
	2/11/16	23785	Ross County Clerk of Courts		280.00	48,688.79
	2/11/16	23786	Clermont County Clerk of Courts - OH		200.00	48,488.79
	2/11/16	23787	Lucas County Clerk of Courts - OH		275.00	48,213.79
	2/11/16	23788	Clermont County Clerk of Courts - OH		300.00	47,913.79
	2/11/16	23789	Stark County Clerk of Courts - OH		523.00	47,390.79
	2/12/16		Water Co., The		10.00	42,040.79
	2/15/16	PR0215	Payroll Co.		58.50	41,982.29
	2/15/16	PR0215	Payroll Co.		6,577.80	40,876.09
	2/15/16	PR0215	Payroll Co.		1,106.20	34,298.29
	2/16/16		Chase		5,219.78	29,078.51
Total 10010- Firm #xxxxxxx				24,949.17	21,304.93	29,078.51

13,825.45	Deposits Waiting to Clear
42,903.96	Sub Total
0.00	A/P
0.00	P/R
-4,820.80	AMEX
-767.00	Chase #0310
37,316.16	Total Balance

Figure 6: Snapshot of Cash in Bank

other things unique to plaintiff law firms.

The last one is my least favorite, you guessed it—your balance sheet. I mean, if one side always equals the other side no matter what you do—assets always equal liabilities—what's the use of it? All kidding aside, I really don't believe many attorneys ever study this document because most have no idea what it's there for.

As I indicated, I'm no expert in accounting, but I can tell you basically that there are items law firms have on their books that will not show up on their P&Ls. Therefore, if you are getting only your P&Ls, you won't see them. For example, any case costs you advance on behalf of a client may be on your balance sheet as in an asset account, not an expense. This is because you are expecting to recoup these in the future. Similarly, if you have any debt or lines of credit or unpaid credit card bills, the amount you owe and payments you make will show up only on your balance sheet.

So whether you understand why balance sheets always balance or not, it will do you some good to review the accounts on your balance sheet to catch any irregularities. You may see some positive or negative balances that seem out of whack to you, and you can inquire and make any corrections needed.

PART IV

TAKING YOUR MARKETING TO THE NEXT LEVEL

CHAPTER 19

Stop Following the Herd

How to Differentiate Yourself Using These Proven, Direct-Response Marketing Principles

Okay, now that the holes in your bucket are plugged, you're ready to spend some additional money on expanding your marketing reach! Marketing is the most misunderstood and misused tool lawyers have in their arsenal. Almost everyone has an opinion about what is good or bad marketing, but virtually no one has ever studied the subject, read a single book about marketing, or has any experience investing their own money in a marketing campaign and measuring its success or lack thereof. Their neck has never been in the noose.

Most people think good marketing is the creative, funny, and silly ads we see during the Super Bowl. If you think about it, the ads aired during the Super Bowl don't ask you to pick up your phone and call for a free consultation, do they? They don't ask you to do anything at the end as a call to action. They don't make any offer. These are simply ad dollars sent out into the marketplace in vast amounts in varying media hoping to slowly sink into your brain so that when you go to the store, you will trust and select their brands and continue to buy their brands—their ads aim at promoting brand loyalty. Those ads are not direct-response marketing ads—they are brand-building ads.

However, you aren't a Fortune 500 company and cannot afford to advertise like one. If you have been running these types of ads and have given up on marketing, I have just identified your problem. If you advertise as the companies who advertise during the Super Bowl do—meaning you run ads with no call to action, designed to build your brand—you're most likely making a huge mistake. Unless you're the 800-pound gorilla in your area spending millions per year on advertising across all media, you cannot afford to spend marketing dollars that do not result in a direct return on your investment. Brand building can be done only as a byproduct of that spend.

The most effective way for a plaintiff's law firm to advertise is by ensuring that every dollar spent returns more dollars than the spend itself. Imagine sending soldiers out into the marketplace whose duty is to come back in one piece with more recruits. This is called your ROI, return on investment. The way to make this happen is to give the person viewing your ad a reason to respond immediately to your ad—your call to action.

Americans are inundated with marketing and advertising messages every day. Some studies suggest that each of us is subjected to up to 5,000 advertisements every day.

Nearly all lawyer ads are filled with the same tired information, the same boasts, and the same lists of features and benefits. Saying, "We care about you!" or "We will fight for you!" just won't cut it anymore. Yelling louder than everyone else won't cut it either.

So how can you expect to get attention? To break through the clutter, you must ask yourself, *Why should anyone choose to do business with me over everyone else and even over doing nothing at all?* One of the critical marketing mistakes lawyers make is failing to differentiate or set themselves apart from their competitors, and that leads to their being lumped in with every other attorney. Unless you're the only game in town, you'll be stuck in mediocrity until you come up with some good answers to that question.

One way to do this is through the use of the ACE principle: Authority, Celebrity, and Expertise. Let's focus on authority and expertise first; I will discuss why celebrity is important in a later chapter. We all want to deal with someone who is an authority on a subject, someone who really knows what he or she is talking about. And that goes hand in hand with someone who has a great deal of expertise—in other words, an expert. By convincing your prospects that you are both of these, you will stand out from the crowd and not have to use offensive, unethical, or dare I say even unprofessional marketing tactics.

A great way to accomplish the Authority and Expertise part of the ACE equation and break yourself out of the boring and ineffective marketing pack is to offer some type of free educational information in all your ads no matter what media you choose. This is something that contains valuable information or guidance you give away for free. What is the root of the word *authority*? You guessed it—author! There is no better way to demonstrate your mastery of a subject than to be an author who has written about it. People have an instant favorable reaction to someone who has written a book about a subject or who writes articles.

Let's go over what this does for you. An information piece:

1. positions you as an expert in your practice niche and brings prestige,
2. clearly and positively differentiates you from your competitors,
3. enables you to build your prospect list as you give this piece away,
4. engenders the recipients' goodwill and trust,
5. helps you educate your prospects and set expectations, and
6. screens out bad prospects by forcing them to self-qualify themselves, saving you time.

Some of the different types of information premiums are books, reports, newsletters, white papers, articles, blog posts, videos, free recorded messages, or even simple checklists. For instance, an attorney might give away a short book to those who have been in an accident on mistakes they should avoid and how they can choose the right lawyer for their cases. Other examples might be in the form of a free report or a checklist on what to do.

"But I don't have anything to write about that's interesting enough that a publisher would want to print," you say. Well, the good news is that in this day and age, there is a little something called self-publishing. You no longer have to wait for a big book publisher to find your idea interesting before you can get an authentic looking and feeling book out into the marketplace. Some companies will help you put the whole thing together, edit it, add graphics, bind it, put it on Amazon and Barnes & Noble, and fulfill the orders for a relatively small fee! You can even find freelancers to write the entire thing for you—something known as ghostwriting. Further, in most cases, we're not talking about a *War and Peace*–sized novel; we're really talking about what amounts to a booklet. Most of the lawyer self-published books used for marketing purposes are under 100 pages of easy-to-read type with lots of white space and room for graphics, photos, etc.

These books are basically made up of the following topics broken down into many chapters:

- all the top frequently asked questions (FAQs) you get along with your best answers
- top mistakes they should avoid
- information to help prospects determine if they qualify for your help

- information about your firm's uniqueness and how you do business
- testimonials, case studies, and stories
- information about fees and costs
- how to really read other lawyers' ads
- how to choose the right lawyer
- a glossary of legal terms
- resources or tools they can get from you to better qualify themselves and make them better clients for you
- what to do next if they think they need help and how to get more information from you

Most of your book has already been written if you have a website or a blog or you write any articles. All you need to do is compile and repurpose this information into a book format and add a few more chapters. You now have a book and a free giveaway!

We will talk about celebrity in the next chapter and how you can use this book to increase the number of leads you receive.

CHAPTER 20

The Marketing Two-Step
How to Generate Maximum Leads

What is 1-step versus 2-step marketing? Lawyer ads that ask people to call in to schedule a free consultation are utilizing the 1-step method. You and your competitors are most likely doing 1-step marketing. Ads that offer an information freemium, such as a free report, are engaging in 2-step marketing. The first step is to get the prospects to take the bait, the free report, in exchange for giving up their contact information. The second step is to eventually get them to take the next step in your conversion funnel, which is usually a free consultation or some type of meeting with the attorney. Because you're likely already familiar with 1-step marketing, let's discuss why and how 2-step marketing works.

Most people don't wake up one morning and say, "I think I'll hire an attorney today." Instead, they wake up with a problem they need to solve and begin looking for information on how to solve it and learn all their options. They ponder it for a while, sleep on it, even hope the problem solves itself. After they spend some time gathering information from friends, family, online, books, webinars, etc., they think about possible solutions, the pros and cons of taking action, and so on.

Because most people procrastinate when it comes to making decisions, this incubation period could last months. Then when they—not you—are ready to start talking with attorneys, they will begin the process of finding one. After they have made the decision to go about finding a lawyer, they become what I call the "now" buyers, the type of people most attorneys fight over. However, as you now know, this is a very narrow part of the overall group of people who are having problems an attorney can solve.

So by offering them information, you can get them into your spiderweb early on in the process. Once they're in there, it's your job to keep them there while they are incubating and fertilize them so when they blossom, they think of you and only you as the best choice. You want to capture them when they are in research mode before they decide to hire an attorney. Then you want to be top of mind when they do decide to hire one so that they choose you.

You do that by continuing to offer them helpful information and staying top of mind. Your follow up will demonstrate your expertise and that you care, creating trust. And by staying in touch with them on a regular basis, they won't have to look very far to find your name and number when they're ready to call you. This is what is meant by top of mind.

You can also use this first step as a self-screening mechanism that saves your staff time answering the questions of unqualified leads and delivering to your firm prospects who are not only ready to move forward but also qualified to do so.

I know what you're thinking now: *You're telling me I need to hound these people to death like some scummy salesperson. I'm a professional, and professionals don't engage in that type of unprofessional behavior!* No, that's not what I want you to do. Dan Kennedy has a saying about this that applies here. He says you want to be a "welcome guest, not an annoying pest." So the first way you do this is by having your prospects raise their hands and tell you they're interested. You did that in step 1; they asked for your educational information. So next, you want to simply continue to feed them in the same way while also including gentle reminders that you're available for consultation by phone at any time.

The best way to structure this back-end follow up is using multiple forms of media. So if you can get full contact information, you can "touch" the prospect using email (with audio and video), phone, mail, and perhaps even text or fax (though there are some strict laws on the last two that may prevent this). You may also be able to use online ads using retargeting technology.

But before you give away this free information, you must remember to get one piece of enormous value in return: your prospect's contact information.

For example, your follow-up sequence may look like this:

- Day 1: Send information product by email or mail.
- Day 2: Send welcome email, remind them that you're available for questions and free consultation any time.

- Day 3: Send email with helpful tools, stories, testimonials, something to watch, top X mistakes to avoid, reiterate a portion in the information piece, offer to answer questions, offer a free consultation, etc.
- Days 5, 14, 30: Make follow-up call to see if they got the information product and if they have any questions. Leave pre-scripted voice mail if no answer.
- Days 7, 10, 17, 24: Send email with helpful tools, stories, testimonials, something to watch, top X mistakes to avoid, reiterate a portion in the information piece, offer to answer questions, offer a free consultation, etc.
- Days 14, 30, 45, 60: Send snail mail piece with a special offer, a free gift, helpful tools, mistakes to avoid, reminder of offer to answer questions, and free consultation. The last letter should create urgency by having a deadline and announcing it is the final notice.
- Monthly thereafter: Add them to your newsletter list.

You're probably thinking, *How in the world am I supposed to keep track of what state each of these leads is in and its next follow-up step?* Here is where a good CRM program can make all the difference. Using the proper software, you can automate each step of this follow-up sequence.

Your next objection is that this is a big delay from the time they contact you until the time they become clients, and you're afraid of losing potential clients. However, what usually happens when using this type of marketing funnel is that you get the same number of now buyers who want to schedule a free consultation right away and engage your firm, but you also get a pile of leads that will mature into clients at different times in the future whom you would not otherwise have received. You get a lot more leads on the front end than you would have received had you offered only the free consultation option, thus attracting only the now buyers.

The other option to test is to offer two different calls to action at the same time, a higher-threshold offer and a lower-threshold offer. One could be a number they can dial to talk to someone as soon as they call to set up an appointment or to get their questions answered for example. The lower-threshold offer is the ability to request the free information you are providing without having to speak to anyone.

With this method of advertising, you'll be able to rest easy knowing that you not only have the now buyers coming in from your ads each month but you also have a huge number of names in your funnel at varying stages all being nurtured and fertilized that are coming due each and every month. After running this for a few months, you won't be able to shut this spigot off even if you stopped your advertising completely—the calls would continue to come in for months!

If you do this successfully over a relatively long time in your market, your brand building will be a byproduct of your highly profitable direct-response marketing, giving you all you could ask for from your marketing. And because you have already plugged all the holes in your bucket, you will be maximizing every marketing dollar you spend and will know your true ROI for each new form of media you test.

CHAPTER 21

Celebrity

Last, why is celebrity important? Look around you at what most people spend their time looking at, reading about, and talking about. Isn't it celebrities? Whether Hollywood stars, sports stars, musicians, or reality TV personalities, that is what most people are interested in. Not only that, they will buy whatever those celebrities buy or endorse. That is why you see celebrities attached to so many ads for national brands these days. Now more than ever, brands are harnessing our obsession with celebrities to influence our buying behavior. We mindlessly spend our hard-earned dollars on their weight-loss programs, fragrances, cars they drive, sneakers they wear, and the mocha lattes they sip—all of which they are most likely being paid to enjoy.

A method commonly used mostly by large companies is a celebrity endorsement. These come in all shapes and sizes; the most common is having a celebrity pitch your firm. However, you can also use the fact that you have celebrity clients or celebrity testimonials in your advertising. These do not have to be national celebrities; they can be people in your local area whom your clients would consider influencers—people on the news, reality TV shows, ex-politicians, singers, actors, business owners, activists, current or former sports stars, and so on. Many of these locally famous people can be "borrowed" in your marketing for surprisingly little compensation. (Don't forget to check your rules of ethics on paid endorsements if you go this route. They may prevent you from doing this in violation of the Bates case, of course ☺.)

Another highly effective method is for you to become the celebrity of your firm in your local market. You aren't a celebrity and will never be one, you say? Wrong! I'm not talking about a national Hollywood A-list celebrity; I'm talking about a celebrity of sorts—a celebrity in your local market area or a celebrity to your customer base.

Do you have any attorneys in your marketplace who appear in their ads regularly on TV and elsewhere? We know all they did was pay for ad time, but to the general population, these attorneys are mini celebrities. After all, if they are on TV all the time, they must be important, right? Couple that with some speaking engagements, a few interviews here and there, some published articles and a self-published book and you're a celebrity.

It's even better if you can find a way to get the media interested in you and keep you in the limelight through constant interviews, press releases, your own ads, etc. At the very least, you appear to potential clients as more of a celebrity than all your competition does, and they will likely hire you for that reason alone.

A number of experts can help you become a local celebrity, but this is admittedly a longer and tougher road to hoe than many of the tactics outlined in this book. However, that should not deter you as this is a competitive advantage that cannot easily be copied. Remember, the harder it looks to your competition, the less likely they will ever try to duplicate it! This goes for your back end follow-up funnel as well. Embrace the complexity.

CHAPTER 22

The Incredible Power of A/B Testing

Using the Power of Simple Tests to Turbocharge Your Results

I still remember the first time someone told me about A/B testing in marketing. My consultant was explaining to me that he had another client who did a ton of online advertising. He had a program that allowed him to make changes to multiple items on his website and send half the traffic to the original page, i.e., the control, and the other half to the changed page, i.e., the challenger. After allowing a sufficient amount of traffic and time to pass, he could scientifically find out which changes improved the conversion rate on the page and which changes did not!

What's more, he could build on the successes over time to skyrocket his conversion rate by adding one successful element on top of another until he had the highest possible converting webpage. He didn't have to guess at anything, and there were no other variables that could explain away the results.

This is the beauty of proper A/B testing. You want all the traffic from the same source over the same period to randomly see different things, half of them seeing A and the other half seeing B. What you don't want is to test version A this month and test version B next month because all sorts of other possible variables could affect the results other than the element you're testing.

Here is the ultimate result of many A/B tests on my law firm's website landing page. This is the page we used to send the traffic to for many of our best-performing pay-per-click keywords.

The first page in figure 7 had a 4.5 percent conversion rate from click to form filled out.

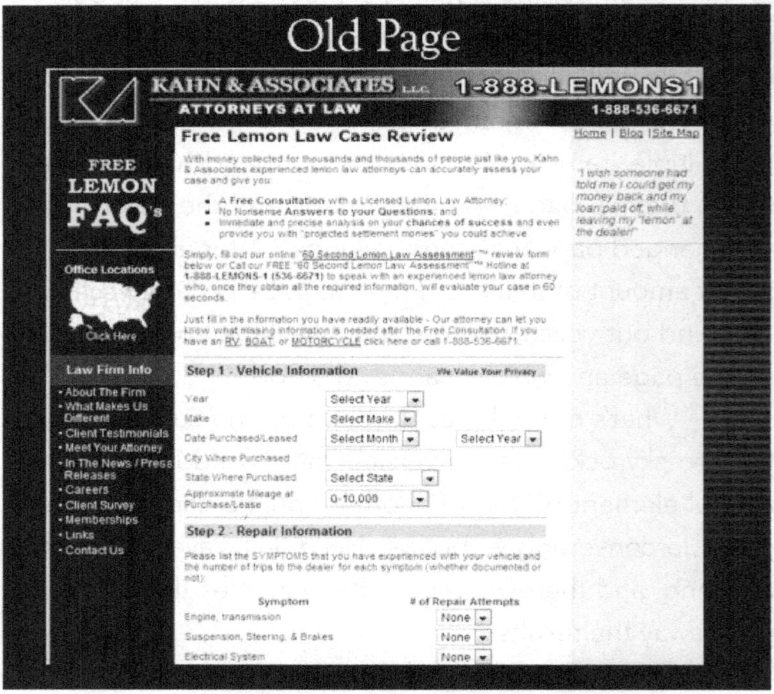

Figure 7: Old Page—4.5 Percent Conversion Rate

After playing with different variables, we ended up with a page that looked like figure 8. This page had between a 9 and a 30 percent conversion rate depending on the state we ran it in. Using 20 percent as an average, that's a 344 percent increase in results! Using real numbers, this means if you have 1,000 clicks per month at a 5 percent conversion rate, you would have 50 leads. If you doubled your conversion rate to 10 percent as a result of your A/B testing, you would receive 100 leads from the same ad spend or twice as many!

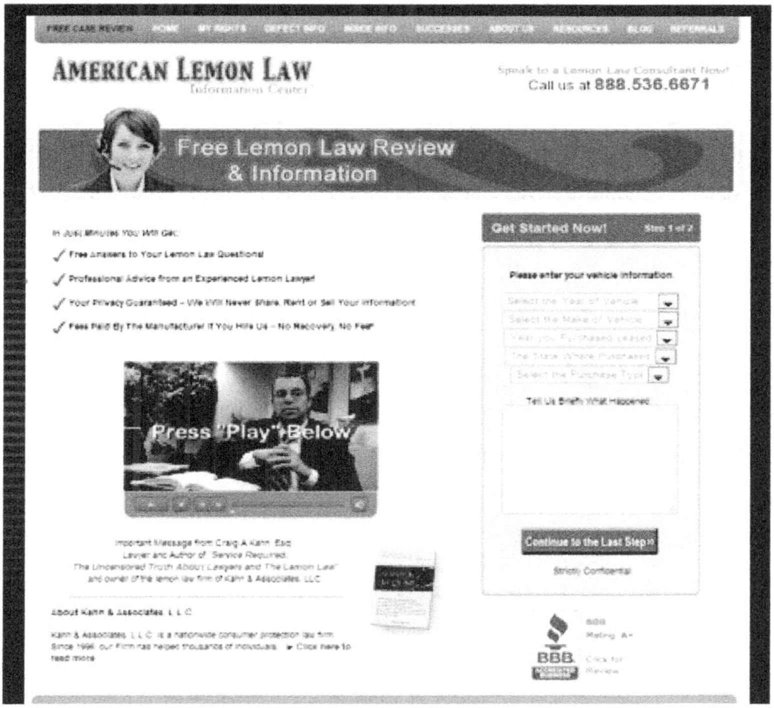

Figure 8: New Page—9 to 30 Percent Conversion Rate

Some of the improvements were a better headline, a good video, benefit-driven copy, an image of the book I wrote, BBB symbol with our A+ rating, and a short, easy-to-use form.

There is a famous story about Tim Ferriss, author of *The 4-Hour Workweek*, and how he came up with the title of his highly successful book. We assume he contracted some high-powered ad agency that did some in-depth research and conducted focus groups to come up with the best title. But no, he didn't do that. He used Google AdWords to run ads with different titles (controlled tests), and whichever one got the most clicks was the winner!

And in a past issue of *Wired* magazine, a man named Dan Siroker, the product manager for Google who now has his own marketing company, told a story about how he showed the Obama campaign how to do what Google relied on in developing and refining its own products every day—the A/B test.

On the Obama campaign page, they started with the button and A/B tested different word choices: Learn More, Join Us Now, and Sign Up Now. Learn More got 18.6 percent more signups per visitor than the default Sign Up Now.

Then they tested a black-and-white photo of the Obama family; it outperformed the turquoise image by 13.1 percent. Using both the family image and Learn More, sign-ups increased by a whopping 40 percent! You can see that sometimes the combination of more than one element can have a compounding effect greater than the sum of the individual results.

They said they were surprised at how bad their instincts had been. For example, they expected a video of Obama speaking at a rally to outperform the still photo. However, the video did 30.3 percent worse than the turquoise image. "Assumptions tend to be wrong," Siroker said.

After all the testing, the rate jumped 140 percent above baseline, and they knew what had caused that. It was estimated that 4 million of the 13 million addresses in the campaign's email list and some $75 million raised resulted from the A/B testing.

You can see why this is so powerful. With online advertising, by constantly testing different elements of your page, you can literally double your business or more and substantially lower your cost per client without spending an extra dime on advertising. The reason is that you will increase the number of people who fill out your form or call you out of those who have already clicked on your ad. While getting more clicks on your ad usually costs you more money, getting more of those people who have already clicked on your ad to take action is free, and the opportunity for improvement is usually tremendous. There are very inexpensive programs available online now that can assist you in performing your A/B tests.

These tests can be done online and offline with equal success. If you're using direct mail, you can split your list into two parts. If you're using print ads, you may have to ask your advertising representative if they can help you, or you may have to resort to the imperfect testing over two different periods. Just make sure to pick similar times of the year when doing this type of testing for best results.

CHAPTER 23

Marketing Math
What's Your Bogey?

"I can't afford that," "That's too expensive," and "I don't want to spend that much" are all phrases that show a misunderstanding of what's known as marketing math. Most lawyers look at the dollars spent on marketing as expenses. If that number on their profit and loss statement is larger this month than last month, they will tell you their expenses have gone up. However, marketing is not an expense when done right—it's an investment. An expense is something that drains a firm's profit, while an investment is something you put money into because you expect it to return more to you than the amount you put in—thus the term return on investment.

If I told you that for every dollar you gave me I would give you three in return, how many dollars would you give me? Would you refrain from "spending" too many one-dollar bills because "It's too expensive?" For example, if you have a pay-per-click campaign that's working, a newspaper ad that's working, and a direct-mail campaign that's working, in many cases, you know with a high degree of certainty that if you put more money into it, it will produce more of the same results you have been receiving. You know that if you spend another $1,000 per month on it, you will receive, let's say, $5,000 in return in the form of attorney's fees. That's a 400 percent return on investment, a 5 to 1 ROI! Where else can you get that kind of return?

When your firm is systematized and your marketing is being tracked properly, you will be able to see this happening; you will be able to determine that certain ads are producing 2 to 1, 5 to 1, 10 to 1 returns on your advertising dollar. And you will be able to "invest" whatever amount you desire to achieve whatever goals you have set for yourself. And if it costs an extra $500 per month to hire an expert to help with some aspect of your marketing but that expert can produce additional cases/clients per month, you will likely see that this is actually a profitable investment, not an added expense.

But you will need to know more than your ROI to really know if a marketing channel is a good one. You will need to know the maximum amount you can afford to spend on each case (your max cost per case) and still make an acceptable net profit.

Digging a little deeper, once you know what your baseline conversion rate is from lead to case, you will then be able to figure out what your cost per lead is both now and in the future if you were to spend more. Your reports should be able to show you both numbers, allowing you to be sure that you are not paying more per lead and ultimately more per case than your firm can afford.

For example, let's say your average fee is $2,000 per case. If you spend $10,000 on a marketing campaign that produces ten cases, you've spent $1,000 per case; that leaves only $1,000 to cover the rest of your expenses and you. Out of that half of your fees, you need to pay for your entire firm's expenses as well as your salary or guaranteed payment. Does that leave you enough money or not?

Here is how you figure that out. Let's assume the following figures:

- You retain 100 cases.
- You earn an average of $2,000 per case—total revenue $200,000.
- You spend $150,000 per year, not including your pay and overhead but including $30,000 per year on marketing.
- You get paid $50,000.

Simply take that $30,000 in marketing expense and divide it by 100 cases and you arrive at a maximum cost per case of $300. If you spent more than that per case, you won't be able to take home $50,000. For example, if you started to see your cost per case rise to $400, you would have to spend $40,000 to get the same 100 cases. If you can get your spend down to less than $300 per case, you will be able get the same 100 cases at less than $30,000 in total marketing spend and you will be able to take home more! You will be spending less than $150,000 per year out of $200,000 in revenue, leaving you with more money.

So your bogey, or maximum cost per case, is $300.

Now you can use this as your test measurement for any marketing channel or newfangled shiny object that is thrown at you to spend your marketing dollars on!

Next time you're presented with a dollar figure for a new ad, campaign, expert, vendor, or anything related to marketing, ask yourself what the ROI on this investment will be, not how much will it "cost" you. If you test it and the returns fit your tolerances, it's a wise choice. If not, you may make some more tweaks and test again, but you can then pass knowing it's the right decision.

CHAPTER 24

Where Should You Market?

I remember making a big mind-set shift when I first started working with a business consultant. In the past, when faced with a decision, for example a decision about where to spend marketing dollars, we would sit around and debate whether it was a wise investment and whether we "thought" it would work. One of the reasons I hired a business consultant was I felt that one of the benefits of working with a business consultant who had been there, done that, was that I could bounce these types of questions off him and he would know the answers! Wouldn't that be wonderful? But I was initially unhappy to find out he basically didn't have any better answers about whether we should try a particular marketing strategy than I did. He did, however, understand the power of a controlled experiment.

When I would ask my consultant whether he thought we should try X, he would respond, "I don't know. Let's test it." Or sometimes, "I don't know. Let's ask your staff what they're seeing and hearing." Or "I don't know. Let's take a survey of the next twenty leads or clients and see if they would do X." And he was right—we could learn far more from inexpensive controlled tests and surveys of clients and staff who were in the trenches than we could by merely guessing.

So if you're wondering whether to run ads on Facebook or in your community newspaper, simply run a small test and see if you get any responses. Or better yet, run more than one type of ad and see which one does the best. If it shows promise, invest more and see how good you can make it. If it completely strikes out, double check that all of the pieces of your experiment were working and that you were using proven copy from past ads, and if it all checks out, this may not be a good source for you at the time. But at least you will know for sure. You'll likely stumble across some areas you didn't think would work, that do work, and some that don't work that you thought would work.

You should have some money set aside each year in your budget for marketing experimentation like this. Some of this money will be lost on failed experiments, but that's the cost of doing business or you could say dollars invested in "research and development." Don't let that stop you because over time, the amount you gain from the winners will more than pay for the losers.

CHAPTER 25

The Worst Number in Marketing
Panning for Marketing-Channel Gold

According to Google, a safari is an expedition to observe or hunt "animals" in their natural habitat. Your goal is to go on your own safari—not for animals but for profitable marketing channels. You are hunting for these using two of your new tools: 1. alternative direct-response marketing calls to action and 2. Your max cost per case.

Your goal should be to find as many channels as possible that meet your new cost-per-lead/case test. The obvious reason is that the more you have, the more clients you can retain and the more profitable your law firm will be. The second but less-obvious reason is that the more successful channels you have, the more stable and predictable your business will be. This is because you have no control over some channels, and they can be severely cut off by forces beyond your control.

For example, there was a time when businesses were making a killing by faxing solicitation letters until the federal government banned it. The same goes for telemarketing. Commercial telemarketers are regulated by federal and state laws that establish curfews, do-not-call lists, and other requirements aimed at protecting consumer privacy.

Google has blacklisted many companies for their tactics, delisted their sites, or temporarily removed them from the first page with their latest algorithm change. Facebook has taken similar steps.

And sometimes, it's simply a matter of new competition entering a space you once dominated. At one time, we were obtaining over 95 percent of all our cases from our PPC marketing. We had certain states where there were only one or two firms marketing in our space on the PPC results for the best keywords. The cases were gushing in, and things were rosy.

But over time, other firms appeared in our space, the cases began to dwindle, and we began paying more than we wanted to. Some firms that didn't know their numbers as well as we did seemed to bid amounts that were unsustainable. Not having a number of profitable marketing channels for our cases caused us a lot of consternation. I know businesses that literally have dozens of profitable sources of leads. Had we had just a handful, we would have been in much better shape in the short and long term. As Dan Kennedy says, "The worst number in business is the number 1," meaning one marketing channel, one key person, one key vendor, or one of anything. I would add this doesn't apply if you are talking about your place among your competitors of course! Make sure you don't make this same mistake and enjoy your safari!

PART V

GETTING A LIFE AND "QUITTING" YOUR JOB

CHAPTER 26

Getting a Life
How to Remove Yourself from the Billable Hour Treadmill

If you love the actual day-to-day handling of cases, have time for everything, and don't want to change anything, this chapter might not be for you. But I asked you some questions at the beginning of this book to see if you agreed with any of them. If you have read this far, one or more of those questions resonated with you. This section is designed to help you find and free up more of your most precious unrenewable resource—your time. We'll also discuss how to move yourself from a having a job to becoming the owner of an asset—your law firm—that produces income for you.

The solutions to many of these problems are virtually identical. The problems stem from the attitude that because we are lawyers, we have to practice law or we are somehow violating some social contract and that that is where we provide the only or the most value. Couple that with also wanting to be your own boss and you have a recipe for burnout and chaos for most people in private practice.

If you truly want to achieve some or all of the goals I have been outlining herein, you have to first change your mind-set about your role in your law firm. Then you will have to begin implementing many of the suggestions outlined in this chapter.

First, you have to begin to view your law practice as a business, a business that delivers a product called legal services. You are no longer to refer to yourself as a lawyer. You don't merely practice law anymore; you are the CEO of your law firm. Yes, you also have a license to practice law. But you should be striving to have others in the trenches operating the firm and handling all aspects of a docket of cases, so you can be the coach of the team. Your goal is to shed your responsibility for racking up 1,800 billable hours or its equivalent. You may not even practice law in the firm at all anymore if you choose that route.

Dan Kennedy says that as the owner of your business, you have a duty to the shareholders of your business to maximize your profitability and the value of the business. But you're not a public company, you say? You don't have any shareholders? He argues that you are the shareholder and it doesn't matter if you are public or private. Further, this duty extends to your family, employees, and even vendors as they are all impacted by your success or lack thereof. If you are in dereliction of your duty, you should be fired just like anyone else. And this duty attached to you the day you decided to open your own law office.

Think about other types of well-run, highly successful, medium to large businesses; where do you find the founders, owners, or executives of those businesses? Are they down on the factory floor all day making products? Are they out on the truck traveling to the homes every day delivering the products and services? Are they answering the phones and selling customers widgets or answering customers' questions all day long? Of course not. They've hired people who are paid appropriately for those tasks. That is not the highest and best use of a business owner's time and talents. The owner should be steering the ship and doing high return on time invested (ROTI, a Dan Kennedy term) tasks that have the potential to significantly impact revenue growth or expense reduction or increase the value of the business in the short and long term.

The problem with many professions is that the people who own the business are also the people who must perform the service for the business to make money, or so they think. And the people who perform the service are many times the people to whom the customers come for a reason. People like to go to certain doctors, lawyers, CPAs, etc.; they don't think of those people as a nameless, faceless, corporation but as friends in the community who help them with their problems.

However, the beauty of most marketing-driven, volume-based, plaintiff law firms is that the people who come to those firms aren't expecting to see a specific lawyer who will also be the one to handle every task and every phone call on their files. They may be attracted to a certain firm because a specific lawyer is a local celebrity or featured in the marketing, but that lawyer doesn't have to deliver all the legal services to that client, if any.

For example, my name, face, and story appear in most of our advertising. However, I never take any new-client calls, never meet with any new clients, and don't personally handle any of the cases in our office. I oversee the attorneys handling the files, answer questions on difficult issues, and conduct regular audits of our files to ensure they are being handled properly and on a timely basis. But I am not practicing law in the traditional sense at all. And I have never heard a single complaint or frustration, nor have we lost any clients due to their not being "allowed" to deal with me directly.

There was a time when I did talk to every client and handle every detail of every file. That's how I learned what it took to do things correctly each step of the way. However, very early on, I began creating templates and systems designed to allow someone else to do the same thing as I was doing and to prevent any case from getting stalled or any task from falling through the cracks. I then hired and trained the right people on these systems, and they were able to do the same things I was doing. And together, we improved the templates and systems over time.

I created these because very early on, I realized that if I wanted to grow, I had to find a way to leverage myself and make sure the people I brought on were following my best practices. At first, I hung onto a docket of cases and tried to do everything else needed to grow the firm, but I quickly realized the case work was taking too much time away from what I needed to do to grow the business.

In my experience, the firm was not going to grow into a new practice area, add another attorney, or suddenly see a spike in growth of cases large enough to warrant hiring another attorney unless I was driving that growth. I realized that if I wanted the firm to grow and I needed more time to spur that growth, the most time-consuming thing that had to be taken off my plate was some or all of the case work. So I simply hired more legal help to handle much of it. While I still helped on the hard cases and hard questions, I focused more and more of my time and attention on everything else needed to grow the business.

This also makes mathematical sense using Kennedy's ROTI concept. We all have the same amount of time in a day to use for productive purposes. How we go about spending, or more appropriately investing, our time should be an intentional choice based on the return for a given activity.

For example, I could have continued to handle a docket of cases for the firm and worked forty hours a week doing that and brought in let us say $400,000. If we take that $400,000 and divide it by 2,000 hours (forty hours per week times fifty weeks a year), my ROTI would be valued at $200 per hour.[4]

But if I handled no cases and devoted all forty hours to working on growing the business, hiring and managing people, improving our sales, marketing, and business processes and systems, etc., I could create $1,000,000 a year or more in revenue. Divide that by 2,000 hours, we get $500 per hour, more than two times the ROTI!

Even better, once I get the business processes, sales, and marketing systems and software in place and have a great team of people, I will be able to cut my time back significantly due to not having the day-to-day case work. If I worked only twenty hours per week, my return would be $1,000,000 a year divided by 1,000 hours (twenty hours per week times fifty weeks a year). Now I am up to $1,000 per hour or two times the previous ROTI number and five times the original number! My ROTI is a lot more per hour, and I still have twenty-plus hours left to devote to other income-generating activities or for family, charity, and hobbies!

Now, I can choose to get involved in a specific case or to get involved when a case reaches a certain point, but I can also simply choose not to. I work on what I enjoy most in the firm and the areas in which I can have the biggest impact.

For example, let's say you own a business and you have a salesperson who is great at closing. Would you want to saddle that salesperson with research tasks, list-building tasks, appointment-scheduling tasks, even cold calling? Or would it be smarter to have people being paid less who don't have that salesperson's skill set to handle all those tasks so your superstar closer can spend as much time as possible each day having meaningful conversations with prospects who are properly qualified and ripe to be sold? Will the business do better having this salesperson talk to ten or twenty of those people per day and assigning others the miscellaneous tasks associated with the job, or is the business better off saving money by not paying for an assistant and having the closer talk to just a couple prospects per day? The answer is obvious, and there are many parallels found in many plaintiff firms, especially at the owner level.

This critical question must be answered: Where are you most valuable to your law firm? Where are you working at your highest and best use? For example,

- Are you the best trial/appellate attorney, the one who gets the most and highest verdicts? (This is not the same as handling all the tasks on the case.)
- Are you the best rainmaker in the firm, the one who finds all the best referrals and referral sources?
- Are you the best marketer in the firm, the one who thinks of ideas in the middle of the night and enjoys learning about techniques and testing them in the market?

Ask yourself this question and determine if you're fully utilizing the skills you have that add the most value to your firm's bottom line. If you are, look next at all the other responsibilities you've kept control of that are not adding value or you don't like doing and are preventing you from focusing on your highest and best use and delegate them as soon as possible! These are usually tasks like bookkeeping, office management, scheduling, routine hearings and simple legal tasks, client status calls, etc.

The one task that almost every successful entrepreneur will tell you cannot be delegated completely is marketing. You can hire people to leverage you when it comes to implementing marketing ideas, but it's very difficult to find someone to work for you who cares about the firm as much as you do and who can drive the marketing as well as the owner because you will do a far better job at this critical function than just about any employee. Further, many people find that they begin to enjoy the marketing of their business more than just about any other function they could perform in the business.

The most successful business owners realize at some point that what is most important for them to substantially grow their businesses is not for them to be the doers of the services their businesses provide or the makers of the products they sell but to be the chief marketers of those services or products. This mind-set shift can cause exponential growth to occur in almost every instance that sufficient action is taken on it.

To free up time to focus on these high-value activities, you will have to learn to give up control of certain tasks and delegate them. If you are not strong in this area, it's best to take just one small thing at time until you have been able to build up your "risk-tolerance muscle," as Frank McKinney, author of *Make It Big*, would say. Many lawyers are at first very fearful of giving up responsibility for different tasks. The best way to overcome this is to start small and begin to see that virtually no error that occurs is enough to kill your business. Once you see the liberating effect this has on your time and stress and the small number of issues, if any, that arise, you will gain the confidence to delegate more and more critical tasks.

I remember the first office manager I hired and how afraid I was to delegate certain matters to her. Although frustrating for her, we moved very slowly. I had already delegated almost all the legal and paralegal work to attorneys and paralegals, but until that time, I hadn't delegated many of the management tasks I was responsible for. Each item I delegated to her, I continued to watch very closely in the short term. After a while, I realized this was just a waste of my time; she was doing it as well as if not better than I was.

Before too long, I had removed all the drudgery from my job and felt liberated. I could be away from the office without fearing that the business would grind to a halt if any problem arose. And I finally realized someone else could do these things just fine without me. I wasn't as important to the daily functioning of the office as I had thought.

CHAPTER 27

Figuring Out Where Your Time Is Going

In order to start moving down this path, the first thing you need to do is to figure out where your time is going each day. The simplest thing to do is to make a chart (similar to the one in figure 9 on the following page) and put it on your computer home screen or on your desk, and every fifteen or thirty minutes, mark down what you worked on. If you're used to keeping billable hours, you're already doing this. However, you need to also keep track of all the nonbillable things you're doing as well. Make sure there is an extra column on the chart to use to categorize the task later.

After keeping this for thirty days, read through the items and try to label them in the blank column according to the type of task. For example, if it was related to marketing, then put down marketing; if it was related to IT issues, put down IT issues, etc.

	TASKS	TYPE / CATEGORY (try to be consistent with naming)
7:00		
7:30		
8:00		
8:30		
9:00		
9:30		
10:00		
10:30		
11:00		
11:30		
12:00		
12:30		

Figure 9: Time-Tracking Chart

Then add up how much time you are spending on each of these tasks. Divide the total by four to estimate how much time you are spending per week. Then rank the items' demands on your time from most to least. You should have some eye-opening items on this chart by the time you're done. You should see things on your list that the managing partner of a law firm shouldn't be handling.

If the ROTI is way below what you're worth, you are effectively being paid partner wages for office assistant work; that is not a smart way to run any business. Tasks that can be pushed down to a lower level at a lower pay scale must be pushed down. This will free up time for you to work at your highest and best use and allow you to focus on only those tasks where you add the most value. Your time will then be most highly leveraged; you will be doing what a business owner should do.

CHAPTER 28

How to Take Control of Your Time and Calendar

Once you have identified where your time is going and have started to delegate the tasks you shouldn't be handling, the next thing you will need to do to free up your time is take control of your schedule. If you're like most plaintiff law firms, you have zero control over your day; you're running around putting out fires all day. You work on only urgent matters, never getting to work on the important, or only very little as the author of *The 7 Habits of Highly Effective People* Steven Covey would say.

You're not going to like this, but you cannot blame this on the practice of law or on your staff or clients. The reason you have no control over your time is you! I know that sounds crazy, but the reason why your staff comes to you all day with questions and the reason why clients call and email you all day looking for instant answers is because you have trained them to behave that way.

With regard to staff, what happens at your office now when one of them has a question or an issue? Can they email it to you whenever they want? Can they simply knock on your door whenever they want? Think about it. What does an open-door policy mean? Do you have one?

This sounds well and good to the theorists, but the truth is that an open-door policy is a terrible idea if it means that any time anyone on your staff has a problem, challenge, or brain fart of any kind, he or she can interrupt you and ask for your help. This may not be bad with one employee, but what about when you have forty employees and 500 active clients? They have been trained to come see you with anything and everything and not to use their own heads first.

You are arguably the most valuable person in the firm doing the highest and most impactful thinking about marketing, strategy, and problem solving and what direction the firm is heading. But you get interrupted every two seconds because the computer doesn't work, someone needs to leave early, this or that client has questions or is insisting on talking to you now, Jane's radio is too loud—on and on and on.

Fixing this is not just theory on my part. That nightmare scenario doesn't play out at my firm and hasn't for many years. I don't have an open-door policy, and no one is complaining. I try to schedule everything. If you want to see me about something, we schedule it. If I sense it's going to be complicated, I might ask you for the questions in advance so I'll be prepared to discuss the answers during our meeting. Not only am I not interrupted this way, but I am also prepared, the meeting is efficient, and there is no need for a second meeting because I need to think about the answers to the questions from the first meeting. We have a start time and an end time; it's not an open-ended affair.

This is also the way you train your staff not to come to you at the drop of a hat. Require them to bring their questions to you at designated times that are convenient for you. Often, by the time they have their meeting with you, the problem will have been solved and you won't have to do anything.

Many management experts advise that if those on your staff have problems or complaints about something, before they can bring it to you, they must have thought of at least one if not several possible solutions and which one they recommend and why. It is only then that they can bring you complaints about something or raise issues. Your job is to simply ask a few more questions and potentially pick the solution you like best.[5] If you are a new staff member and have many questions or you are one of my managers, I will set up regular meetings with you either daily or weekly. This way, my staff is forced to gather and think about topics as they come up and I handle them all at one predetermined meeting. They are not handled piecemeal as they arise whereby I am interrupted by them.

Another rule we have is that no one is allowed to email me anything sensitive; that includes complaints about someone in the office, a policy, their pay or bonuses, their hours, and so on. The reason for this is that it's much too easy to simply shoot off an email at the slightest offense. If it's important enough for them to bring it to my attention, they need to schedule a time to see me about it personally.

Additionally, it's a terrible idea to ever discuss

anything sensitive by email because inevitably, those who receive your emails will interpret your words in a way that will offend them and that could have been avoided if they could have seen your body language and expressions and heard your tone of voice. Much of the way we communicate as humans is lost in email.

Professor Albert Mehrabian has pioneered the understanding of communications since the 1960s.[6] His research provided the basis for the widely quoted statistics for the effectiveness of spoken communications. He found that:

- 7 percent of the message we receive has to do with the words that are spoken
- 38 percent of the message we receive is paralinguistic (the way that the words are said)
- 55 percent of the message we receive has to do with facial expressions

Therefore, when all you have is an email, you are receiving only 7 percent of the communication—the words themselves. The way they are said, the tone of voice, and the facial expressions are missing. This is the source of what is often a lot of bad feelings and misunderstandings when we use only email and a great reason not to discuss anything sensitive with your staff by email.

With regard to client calls, I know many plaintiff law firms around the country that refuse to take any unscheduled client calls absent a real emergency and refuse to answer any client email immediately. And as you know, there are very few real emergencies for most of our clients; they just think they are emergencies. They simply explain this to the clients at the time of engagement and make them sign off on it and then remind them of their communication policy regularly in their monthly newsletter, email signature blocks, letterhead, and other ways. They have trained their clients to behave a certain way.

Clients need to be taught that a law firm does not operate the same way as, for example, a retail store. The lawyers are not just standing around waiting to take their calls. Lawyers need time to focus and prepare, review documents, read case law, and attend court appointments, depositions, trials, etc. Clients must fit into the lawyers' schedules, not the other way around. And most clients understand this once you explain to them that surely they want their case treated the same way by their lawyer should another client call while the lawyer is working on their case. They would not want their lawyer distracted by someone else's call to the detriment of their case.

At many well-run firms, as well as other businesses, the owner's entire day is scheduled ahead of time. They block off time not only for court hearings but also for client calls, even for sending and receiving emails. The owners have time blocked off for answering staff questions, meetings, and for working on the business, for example, to handle marketing-related tasks.

Last, avoid phone tag whenever possible; it's a huge waste of time, and the frustration it causes adds to your stress throughout the day. If you need to speak to someone by phone, either you or your assistant should ask the person what time would be good for you to call and book this on both of your calendars. This is super easy with programs such as Outlook and Google Calendar as you can "invite" the other person with a click of a button and it will add the calendar item to both of your calendars, ensuring there is no confusion. Now when you call them, they will be waiting for your call the first time you call, not the fifth!

Additionally, this allows you to be fully prepared for the call as you can pull out and review key information just prior to the call, making your performance on the call much better and likely that of the other person as well, creating more efficiencies.

CHAPTER 29

Steering the Ship
How to Get Everyone Moving in the Same Direction

Once you have all of these systems in place and you have reports telling you what's happening in your law firm, the next step is to steer your ship in the direction you want. As the captain, you need to chart a course to your destination. You must figure out what your key metrics or your key performance indicators (KPI) are reading now and what they need to read for you to reach your goals. You need to begin to watch them daily and take action around every one of them to improve and grow. And you need to publish a few of them for your team to see and strive to reach each month.

A common way of handling this at a law firm would be to set a gross revenue and net income target for the upcoming year and work backward from there. For example, once you know your revenue targets, you can then figure out how many cases/clients you need to handle, how many settlements, if applicable, what average fee per case/client you need, and how many appointments and leads this would take using current conversion percentages. Each of these would be one of your metrics or KPIs.

You should also set firm goals for things that are important to your success. In my firm, the most important figures are the new-client engagements and the settlements. We have new-case goals, settlement goals, and a few others. I take the total number of cases for the year that produce the income totals we are seeking and divide by twelve months to get the monthly new-case goal. After backing out our close-file rate or those files for which we will have zero recovery, I can then set a goal for the number of settlements we need per month on average to achieve our revenue goal. I remind my staff that we don't get paid anything unless and until the case is resolved.

We then publish this number in a way that everyone can see it and work toward it. Remember, a law firm, like any business, needs money to remain in business, pay the people who work there, and fairly compensate the risk-takers and shareholders—the owners. To do that in my firm, we need to retain and settle a certain number of new clients each month. Everyone is of course reminded that these goals are to be achieved within the ethical limits of a law firm. But using that as our guide, everyone knows what the firm is trying to achieve and can see our progress almost minute by minute.

Just like the captain of a ship, now that I know where I'm going, I can make course corrections on the fly depending on what I'm seeing. If any of my key metrics starts to drop, I can see it and begin asking questions of the proper personnel to find out what the problem is. Once we are able to identify it, we can begin making corrections until this number is back to where it's supposed to be. This is much harder to do if you're overwhelmed with tasks you should not be handling.

When we hit our targets for the month or the quarter, we will have some type of celebration. We may shut down early on Friday and let everyone have a longer weekend, or simply bring in or go out for lunch, or my favorite, shut down early and head to the bar for happy hour!

Does the thought of doing that make you feel squeamish? If that's the case, ask yourself why. Why does a law firm have to be different and feel like a morgue every day? When you reach firm goals, is there anything wrong with celebrating? The people who work at a law firm are no different from those who work anywhere else; they want to be part of something meaningful and enjoy their work and workplace. Well, celebrating your success is an important part of satisfying those basic human needs. This is another mind-set shift that could hold you back if you disagree.

As I see good things happening, I will publicly praise certain individuals or teams in person or by a firm-wide group email for a job well done. Almost always, other members of the team will chime in and say kudos as well. If you have the right people on your bus, you will find that your team will pay very close attention to these goals and will take pride in making sure they are living up to expectations.

Furthermore, there are no surprises at the end of the year about how the firm performed. So if you have an off year and have to tell your staff you don't have a lot of bonus money available, they won't be surprised. On the other hand, if you have a great year, you should be prepared to reward them and not be stingy because they will know that the firm did well.

I remember years ago I set some goals for my attorneys to create some friendly competition in the office. One of my attorneys refused to participate in this, saying he felt uncomfortable somehow "betting" on a client's case. These are the types of attorneys who are toxic to your law firm and must be screened out prior to hire. The truth is, every lawyer in a litigation practice has a built-in conflict of interest when a settlement offer is proposed. Whether the firm is short on money that month, bonus money is available, goals are trying to be reached, or a vacation is looming, the lawyer is tempted to recommend a faster settlement than if he or she was operating in a vacuum without any of these real-world competing considerations. The way I see it, every lawyer has conflicting considerations, but he or she must still find a way to represent clients zealously and within the rules of ethics.

However, human nature is such that we may not make that last call at the end of the day or try everything possible to reach the other party or their representative if we don't have any extra incentive to do so. One may not push as hard to speed up trial dates or urge the court to set alternative dispute resolution dates. When done correctly, the result of this is that more clients are helped and helped faster than without this type of program. Most clients just want their cases resolved quickly and fairly. That is the basis of the incentive program we have in place and that I continue to believe in.

For your firm to reach its highest potential, you and your attorneys will have to be comfortable with firm goals and incentive programs designed to maximize everyone's efforts.

PART VI

A FINAL WORD

CHAPTER 30

The *Entrepreneurial* Business Owner's Manifesto

Once upon a time, a young man had a goal to achieve freedom for himself and his family and to be able to live a great life on his own terms. To do so, he left the security and comfort of his salaried job, gathered up all his savings, signed personally on additional financing, and took the personal and financial risk to start his own business.

At first, out of necessity, the owner was not only the visionary and decision maker; he was also responsible for every job in the business—marketing, sales, legal and administrative, customer service, accounting, IT, and all general tasks.

However, his goal was to create a separate entity that generated profit regardless of whether he was present or performing tasks much as if he had owned a rental property. The owner realized that to fulfill his dreams, he needed to grow and needed to delegate all these tasks to a team of great people. The job of the team would be to replace the owner and master these functions in the ways he had set out.

As the business grew, one by one, he added legal assistants and attorneys to help take care of the legal work, the intake, and customer service. He also quickly added accounting help. Eventually, he added key people to manage the other team members and the office.

Again, all these people had been brought in to free up the owner's time, allowing him to work *on* the business instead of *in* the business and to help the owner fulfill his dreams. He focused on the areas of the business he excelled at and enjoyed most and where small investments in time produced the most impact—the vision, direction, and marketing of his business.

Over time, he found that some team members routinely came to him to answer every difficult question or to solve every problem. He found that some people wanted to do things their own way instead of following the owner-approved systems. He found that some people needed constant reminding of projects assigned to them or they would fall through the cracks.

He explained to them that they were not allowing him to realize his vision if they could not do their jobs without relying on him. He reminded them that they were there to replace him. He realized it was important to explain to them that it was okay to make mistakes once but not twice. And he would rather they learn from these mistakes than rely on him for the answers.

He also found that some team members expected the owner to be on-site as much as the team. Others wondered why he didn't just jump in and help take calls, cover hearings, settle cases, and so on like everyone else. Did he think he was better than them? Did he do this just because he was the owner and wanted to show off his power?

To all this, the owner explained that if he did the work of his team, he would be training the team to rely on him to pick up the slack instead of themselves when his goal was just the opposite— to create an asset that ran without the need for him to be there much of the time. This would have the opposite effect over time and would not fulfill his dream.

He believed that some wondered why owners in general who may not have put in as many hours as some team members were entitled to a larger share of the profits. He reminded them that the owner typically has put his own money on the line and signed personally to borrow money from others to start the business and keep it afloat when funds were needed during bad times. Further, in good years, the owner needed to make enough to cover the years he made a poor profit or needed to put money back in the business. If the business went belly-up, the owner stood to lose his investment and would be left to deal with the disgruntled clients, bar association, bank, financiers, lessors, disgruntled employees, lawyers, lawsuits, on and on. The team members would simply walk out with their stuff and find other jobs. But every day, the owner puts himself at risk. Those who disapprove of his actions put nothing at risk. It is he who put his chips on the table and his neck in the noose every day that gets priority. He who takes the risk reaps the rewards.

Further, when anything goes wrong, the owners typically take on this heavy responsibility. For example, when defects occur in cars, do any team members who worked on them come forward and say, "We're sorry. Please dock our pay so the owners and stockholders who invested in and relied on us don't suffer?" No. That falls on the owners and stockholders, which is why they reap the lion's share of the rewards.

After hearing this, some attorneys thought that they too have some liability when things go wrong in a law firm setting. The owner agreed that while that risk is somewhat heightened, it doesn't rise to the same level as the owner's. After all, the business pays for the attorneys' insurance, so it's therefore very unlikely for an attorney to be individually liable. Further, the attorney's risk is on his cases alone and within his control, unlike the owner, who is ultimately liable for all the cases and the actions of the entire team.

He reminded them not to take this the wrong way. It's not that he didn't want the best for his team members and/or didn't want them to succeed. It's not that he thought he was smarter than they were or that he worked harder than they did. It's not that he didn't appreciate all the work they put into their education and all the sweat they put into his business.

Every job done by the team members is important. But profits are shared by the owner in our society by paying salaries, bonuses, benefits, taxes, etc. It's only when those are all paid that the owner gets to keep what's left over. That may be 2 percent for some businesses or as much as 20 percent for others. But it's a long, long way from 100 percent. However, 100 percent of the liability and responsibility is the owner's and owner's alone.

That's why a company's number-one responsibility is not to the customer, but to the shareholders (the owner in a small business). It doesn't mean the customer isn't important, but the people who invest in a company own it, not the team members, not the suppliers, not the customers, and not the community.

The team members are there to allow him to do the things he is best at and enjoys doing the most and where he can make the most revenue for the business in the least amount of time. Therefore, the owner's goal is to work on things that are important but not urgent. If he must deal with the crises of the day, he will never be able to see the big picture and steer the ship. And at the end of the day, one way team members can determine whether they are succeeding in their positions is to simply ask themselves whether their job performance is helping the owner fulfill his dreams or in some way frustrating his pursuit of them.

IN CONCLUSION

You should never forget who owns your law firm and the risk you take every day; it's you, not your staff. I encourage you to make your staff feel that they are part of the decision-making process and seek their input on matters they have expertise in, but at the end of the day, you must make decisions that are in the best interests of the shareholder(s), not your staff. It's your business, and it's designed to serve your lifestyle.

Remember, as you come across concepts being used in other businesses, smart attorneys ask, "How can I apply this to my business?" They don't say, "That will never work in my business." Don't be one of the excuse makers who says, "My business is different." It's not.

AFTERWORD

HOW TO GET HELP FROM ME

I am happy to take on a handful of attorneys who would like to work with me directly to create the business of their dreams, attorneys who want to take the ideas presented in this book and systematically implement them in their firms.

However, this program is not for everyone, and I do not work with just anyone. I take on only a few ideal candidates because my time is limited and I want each one to see massive results. If you have any interest in this type of coaching, simply email me at ckahn@kahninteractive.com for a copy of my Profit Maximization Application.

Once that is complete, we will schedule a fifteen-minute free strategy session to help us determine if you and your firm are right for me and if I am the right person for you.

Also, if you have any questions, comments, or just some feedback on this book, you can always reach me at ckahn@kahninteractive.com.

Good luck with your firm, and may all your dreams come true!

To your success,

Craig A. Kahn, Esq.

END NOTES

1 A mastermind is an alliance of like-minded people working together toward a common definite object. It's based on Napoleon Hill's *Mastermind Group*, discussed in his book *Think and Grow Rich*.

2 Morgan, Thomas D. (2005) *Legal Ethics*, 145. Thomson-BarBri. ISBN 0-314-15633-X.

3 Wikipedia, "Bates v. State Bar of Arizona."

4 I will use Gross Revenue numbers for purposes of this example even though it may be more appropriate to use Profit or Owners Discretionary Income or Net Income to define what portion of this revenue is actually beneficial to the Owner.

5 This is the focus of the book *The One-Minute Manager* by Kenneth Blanchard and Spencer Johnson.

6 Albert Mehrabian received a PhD from Clark University and in 1964 commenced an extended career of teaching and research at UCLA. He currently devotes his time to research, writing, and consulting as professor emeritus of psychology at UCLA. Mehrabian's work featured strongly (mid to late 1900s) in establishing early understanding of body language and non-verbal communications.

WA

Made in the USA
Monee, IL
04 November 2026

67384898R00105